OPTIONS STRAT

MW00981731

Simplified Strategies to Create A Passive Income on Options. Tips and Tricks on Stock Market, Day Trading, Money Management and Trading Psychology.

or professional advice. The content within this book has been derived from various sources. Please consult a licensed professional before attempting any techniques outlined in this book.

By reading this document, the reader agrees that under no circumstances is the author responsible for any losses, direct or indirect, which are incurred as a result of the use of information contained within this document, including, but not limited to, — errors, omissions, or inaccuracies.

Introduction

Chapter 1. Writing Options and Earned Income

Chapter 2. Before You Enter a Trade

Chapter 3. Creating Your Own Day Trading Strategy

Chapter 4. Candlestick Common Patterns

Introduction

If you want to be successful with trading, you need to know how to organize your trading day effectively so that you are able to get everything done in a timely manner. Having a proper routine for your trades will ensure that you are consistent in everything that you do which will support you in maximizing your profits from your trade deals.

Although each trader will go about their daily routine slightly differently from the next, every trader approaches their daily routine in roughly the same way. You should start with this basic trading routine and adapt it as needed while you grow to ensure that you are getting the most out of your routine.

I strongly advise that you keep a separate notebook where you can track your tasks, findings, and thoughts as you go about your daily routine to ensure that you are staying focused and organized. This will also help you reflect later on to identify ways that you could possibly improve or streamline your routine so that you are even more effective in the marketplace.

Pre-Market Tasks

What you do before the market opens is crucial to your entire trade day. Most traders will begin their days around 6 AM EST, as this gives them plenty of time to get their day prepared before the market opens. The more prepared you are in advance, the better you will be able to utilize your time once the market opens to conduct actual trades and position yourself for maximum profits.

Before the market opens, there are four tasks that every single trader will engage in to help them get prepared for the day ahead.

These include conducting a market overview, locating potential trades, designing their watch list, and checking their existing positions. We are going to discuss how each of these tasks occurs so that you can get a feel for how you can build the beginning of your trade day around these strategies.

Market Overview

The first thing you need to do is conduct a market overview which will allow you to catch up on what has happened overnight. Stocks have a tendency to change overnight, so paying attention to this information is key in helping you lie the foundation for your trades ahead. Once you know where the market is at, you can get a feel for how that might be influencing your existing trades and how it might affect the next trades you plan on making.

The easiest way to conduct a market overview is to check out a news platform like CNBC or MarketWatch, as these have a tendency to provide the best and most recent information regarding the stock market.

You want to pay attention to the overall market sentiment, the sector sentiments, and the current holdings. For the market sentiment, you want to see whether the general market is bullish or bearish, get a feel for what the key economic reports are and pay attention to inflation and currency.

For sector sentiments, you want to pay attention to which sectors are trending and growing right now, as these are going to give you an idea as to where you may make the most profit with your trades. You also want to pay attention to any news, earnings, and SEC filings that may impact your current holdings as these might influence your next move with your trade deals.

Locating Potential Trades

Once your foundational information is laid down for the day, you want to take a look for where you could position yourself for potential trades. As a swing trader, you want to take a look for fundamental catalysts which will indicate where the most profitable positions are for you in the market. Generally, there are two ways that a swing trader will look for fundamental catalysts through special opportunities and through sector plays.

You can also watch for chart breaks, although these are not always as easy to find.

In looking for special opportunities, you want to pay close attention to SEC filings and, sometimes, headline news. This information will give you an idea as to what is going on in certain stocks allowing you to find special opportunities to get into a new deal and profit on it, and they can also help you avoid big losses on possible deals.

The special opportunities you want to pay attention to will be linked to SEC filings and will include circumstances such as initial public offerings (IPOs), insider buying, bankruptcies, buyouts, mergers, takeovers, acquisitions, and restructurings. Essentially, any major event that affects a company is going to be reason enough for the stocks to shift which could create a perfect opportunity for you to jump in and profit from that stock.

Sector plays can be found by paying attention to the news and reputable financial information websites that will help inform you as to which sectors are performing the best. By finding the sectors that are performing the best, you can start looking for great opportunities to buy into options that will secure your profits from that trending sector.

Sector plays can be harder to analyze as you need to predict how far the trend is going to go before the market corrects itself, but if you can play them properly they yield much higher returns than virtually any other strategy out there.

As per usual in the stock market, the higher the reward the higher the risk, so do be cautious when getting into these deals. Make sure that your decision is based on logic and reasoning and not based on all of the news your hearing about this particular sector.

Do your research, even when research seems unnecessary due to all of the coverage a certain sector might be getting so that you can trade with confidence and protect yourself against possible risks.

If you want to also take the time to look for chart breaks, this can help you find additional opportunities to get into the market and make trades. These chart breaks are exclusive to swing traders and serve as a great opportunity for you to get into the market and earn a quick profit off of a trade deal.

Chart breaks typically represent a stock that has been heavily traded and that is near a key resistance level which means that it is about to swing into the opposite direction. Swing traders look for these patterns to identify where the stock is either going to breakout or breakdown so that they can earn a profit with their stock. Chart breaks are only important if there is enough interest in the stock, however, as stocks with not much interest will be unlikely to yield enough action to significantly swing it in either direction.

Creating Your Watch List

As you go through possible positions, you want to be building your watch list. Your watch list is comprised of all of the possible positions you could take and the research you have backing up that particular trade option. This is a simple sheet you can write up each day that will ensure that you do not forget about a great option due to having seen so many different possibilities. Some swing traders will use a dry erase board to create their watch list whereas others will use a notebook to track everything. Personally, I use a dry erase board because I already have so many notebooks going with trading that it is simply easier to be able to write it out, refine it, and erase it at the end of each day.

While you build your watch list, make sure that you track important information such as what the opportunity is, what your entry price should be, what your target price should be, and what your stop-loss price should be.

In other words, you want to track what price you would buy in at, what price you would hope to sell at, and what price you would sell at if the market started going out of your favor. Keeping track of all of this information will help you track each possibility and compare them against each other so that you can make the best decision for what position you will actually enter when the time comes.

Checking Existing Positions

The last thing that you need to do before the market opens is to check your existing positions. You need to make sure that you are fully aware of how all of your existing trades are performing and what you might need to do in order to improve the effectiveness of a trade. When swing trading with options, checking existing positions is going to give you the best opportunity to keep track of how much longer your trades are going to be active for and when you should be planning on engaging in new trades.

In addition to checking exactly where your current active trades are and how they are behaving right now, you will also want to check back through platforms like CNN and Google News to see if there is any information available that may impact your trade.

Being fully aware of what is going on in the world that could impact your trades will help you decide what to do with those trades and how to proceed with managing and closing them when the time comes.

Market Hours Tasks

Once the market opens, you are ready to get into action and put all of your foundational research to work. This is the time where you will be watching to see if your possible positions remain in favor of your goals, and actively trading your stocks. With trading options, you will be watching for options that have expired and options that you may be ready to act on so that you can leverage them for profits. As soon as the market opens, you are able to begin acting on those trade deals, so pay close attention and be ready to move in on those positions that you have highlighted for yourself in your pre-market research.

If you are going to be entering a trade on that particular day, make sure that you are paying attention to the exact right entrance time. This will take some practice to identify where that sweet spot is, but you really want to be on the lookout for it.

Entering a trade at the exact time is your key to earning maximum profits from that trade, so you need to be on the lookout. Entering your trades will always be a variable that requires practice and a little bit of luck, however, managing and exiting your trades should always be an exact strategy that you execute the same way every time.

After-Hours Market Tasks

After-hours is generally not a time where any trades are conducted because the market is not favorable for any trades at that point. The only task you should be focused on completing after hours is reviewing your performance for the day so that you can improve on your skills every single day.

Performance evaluations should include looking for where you performed your best and looking for where you could have performed better.

Knowing where your strengths and weaknesses are will help you decide exactly how you can adjust your strategies on entering, managing, and exiting future trades. With this information, you can decide what parts of the strategy you are going to keep the same, and why, and what parts of your strategy you are going to adjust for better performance results including why and how you will adjust them. It is important that you are thorough in your review as you want to refine your strategy down to an exact science as much as possible which will allow you to guarantee as many profits from your trade deals as possible.

Before you end your day, you should also take one last review of how your open trades are performing. This is going to help you compare them against your morning review while also giving you an idea as to how they have fluctuated, and what that might mean for other trades, overnight when you review them again in the morning.

Chapter 1.   Writing Options and Earned Income

Now we are going to take a look at options from a different angle. Up until this point, our focus has been on buying and then trading options on the market. But there is another way to make money using options if you are somebody who owns shares of stock. And as we will discover, it turns out you don't need to actually own the shares of stock in order to make some money. Although, you will want to keep in mind that some of the possibilities we are going to examine are riskier than others.

If you recall, when you buy an option, you pay a *premium* for it. Now, you have good chances that when you buy an option during your regular trading, you are probably buying it from somebody who bought it from somebody else and so on. But at some point, someone sold to open the option. So, whoever purchased it, from the writer of the option, paid them the premium, which the seller could use as their own income. Selling options can be a nice way to make a good monthly income.

There are a couple of different ways that you can go about doing this. The first way is to actually own the shares of stock that you use as collateral to cover the option. Remember that there is a chance that an option might be exercised. So that possibility is always there. And if you don't own the shares of stock or have money to cover a purchase, it could be a real problem.

Certain people sell options that then they don't even own the underlying stock for, or have the financial backing to purchase shares, and these are called *naked calls* and *naked puts*.

When it comes to selling options, you have to think not only about whether it is a call option or a put, but you also have to consider whether or not it is covered or naked. Either way, the primary goal in most cases is to make income via monthly or weekly payments from selling options. Let's get started by looking at the simplest case, which is a covered call.

Covered Calls

A covered call works in the following way. The seller of the covered call owns at least 100 shares of the underlying stock. People may be speculating that the price of the stock is going to go up. But you can always take a chance if you think that the stock is not going to go up as much as somebody who is trading options is hoping it will go up. Although the price of an *out of the money* call is not going to be the best price that you could get for an option, the fact that it is out of the money cuts the risk that you will lose your shares if someone exercises the option. Secondly, time decay will work in your favor, since as time passes, if the option remains out of the money, it becomes worthless to the buyer. This might seem a bit confusing at first, so let me give you an example.

Suppose that there is a stock that is trading at $100 dollars a share. Consider selling a slightly out of the money call using shares that are already owned to cover it. In this case, we could choose a strike price that is a little bit higher than the market price for the stock right now. For this example, I will choose a $102 strike price with a 30-day expiration date. The price of the option is $2.57. So, if we had 100 shares, we could make $257 by selling the option. If you had 1,000 shares, you could sell 10 options contracts and make $2,570.

But remember there are risks involved in any financial transaction. In this case, the risk is actually fairly low. It is possible that the price of the stock will rise and go above $102, over a 30-day period. And it is also possible that somebody will choose to exercise their option to buy the shares if that happens. Even if they don't, if it goes in the money, the broker can still exercise the option.

Of course, most of the time, stock prices don't fluctuate all that much. But let's say that the price rose to $103. In this situation, it is possible, although certainly not guaranteed, that somebody might exercise the option. If they did so, you would have to sell your shares at $102 per share. But you can buy an option back if necessary as a way to get out of that kind of trouble.

The stock was trading at $100 dollars per share when you wrote the option, so really you are selling the stock at a higher price, and this is not that big of a deal. You are missing out on the $1 higher price that you could have sold the stock at, had you not written the options contract.

However, you sold the option for $2.57. Then you sell the shares for $102, which is a gain of $2 per share. Now add on the $2.57 per share that you got from selling the options contract, and we are up to $4.57 in earnings per share. So, although you lose a theoretical dollar, had you sold the stock on the open market, which brings us down to $3.57, you still made a profit. Of course, we are not taking into account commissions, but overall that won't have that much impact.

When it comes down to it, the actual risk involved is not really selling the stock. Yes, you are giving up a little bit of upside, but you are also still earning money. The real risk is getting in a situation where you are forced to sell shares of stock that you don't really want to sell.

In fact, that is how these options got their name as "calls." The old lingo was that your shares could be "called away" if somebody decided to exercise the option. That is why they are known as *calls*.

In addition to the risk that you might be giving up a future upside, there are other things to consider. If the stock pays dividends, there could be a risk involving the dividend. In simple words, if it is a dividend-paying stock, you have to keep track of the *ex-dividend date*. This is so that you don't get into a situation where somebody exercises their option to buy the shares, and you have to let go of the shares while also giving the buyer the dividend. So, you are probably going to want to look at the ex-dividend date and wait until that date has passed before selling to open against your shares.

Now, in the event that the stock price stays about the same or even declines, then you are in a situation where there is no risk at all. So, using our example if the stock dropped to $99 dollars a share, or even stayed about $100 a share, the option would end up expiring worthless. In that case, you keep the money you earned from the premium, and then you also keep the shares. So, if you are hoping to keep the shares for a long-term investment, then you are all good. You can then repeat the process and earn more premium by writing more options contracts based on the stock.

Some of the things that we can say about this strategy is that it is not the kind of trade that is going to cause you to lose your life savings. The worst thing that could happen is that you may have to sell the shares of stock and miss out on the little bit of profit that you could have made, should the price of the share boost way beyond the strike price. But you are still going to come out ahead financially even though it might not be as good as you could have come out. And you will have to figure out something else to do with the money once you have the shares called away. It is all money that can be reinvested.

Since the risk is relatively low for this type of transaction, brokerages allow level one traders to sell covered calls. For those of you who don't own 100 shares of any stock, unfortunately, that won't be an option for you. But if you do own some shares and you are willing to take some risk in losing the shares, then this could be a way to generate some monthly income.

ONe WeeK options

Some people sell options that expire in as little time as a week because that can minimize the risk a little bit. The reason is that it has less time for the stock to go beyond the strike price and with only a week left on the option, the extrinsic for time value is decaying rapidly.

There are some other possibilities. You can do what is called a close-out. This means that you purchase the call options back, and as a result, your position is closed out. In this case, you might gain or lose money, depending on what the price of the option is at the time you buy it back. But doing this will allow you to retain your ownership of the stock. If the option is still out of the money, it will be much cheaper than you sold it for, so this won't eat into your profits very much.

There is also the possibility of doing what is called a rollout. So, what you do in this case is you buy back the covered calls and then you sell new ones that have the same strike price, but a longer expiration date. So, if you sold covered calls that expired on May 31st, when getting a rollout you would buy them back before they expire and then sell new ones with the same strike price that expired for example on June 30th.

Roll out and up means that you do the rollout strategy, but instead of keeping the strike price the same, you sell the new options with a higher strike price. Conversely, roll out and down is when you use the rollout strategy, but you sell with a lower strike price.

For people who are not too risk-averse, there is also another possibility that of selling call options with a strike price which is actually below the trading share price. Now, why would you want to take that risk? Because the options sell for a much higher price. Let's look at a quick example.

Suppose that your stock is trading at $100 a share. You could sell a call option that expired in 30 days with the strike price of $90 for $10.45 a share. So that would get you a pretty nice premium payment of around $1000 for every options contract that you sold. However, the problem is somebody could exercise their right to exercise the option. That is because the $90 strike price is going to make that pretty attractive when the stock is trading at a hundred dollars a share. So, the risk is real and higher than it would be had you sold a slightly out of the money option. But maybe you are willing to take that risk. For comparison, if you sold it with a $103 strike price, the option would only sell for $2.19, which is definitely less money.

Naked Call

The next strategy is called a "naked" call. This means that you open a position by selling a call that is not backed by the underlying stock. This is a very high-risk move, but it could also be extremely profitable. To sell naked calls, you are going to have to be a higher-level trader, and you are also probably going to be required to have cash in your account because you might need to buy the shares. The risk is that if the option goes in the money and it's exercised, you will have to buy high and sell low.

Suppose that you sell a naked call with an amount of $101 when the stock is trading at $100. Suppose that the company announces they invented a cure for cancer, and the shares jump to $200 a share. In that case, the risk that the option is going to be exercised is going to be pretty high, since a trader could buy the shares from you at $101 a share, which is $99 less than the market price. So, you would be forced to buy the shares at $200 on the market since you did not own them and then sell them to the buyer of the option at $101 a share. An option contract forces the seller to dispose of the shares by selling at the strike amount with no other considerations. So, if you sold one naked options contract in this scenario you lose $99 a share on 100 shares for a total loss of $9,900.

Of course, you will have to weigh everything when deciding whether or not it is worth taking the risk, in most cases, stocks are not going to fluctuate in price as much as we have described here, especially over the limited time periods of most options. So that means there are good chances of you selling naked calls and earning profits from the premiums without much risk of having the option exercised. But it could happen, and you could definitely lose a lot of money.

Most junior traders do not have a high enough level designation to execute this kind of trade, and you will need a large amount of money in your account or use margin. Losses, in theory, could be infinite. So, the "textbook" level of potential losses for this type of strategy, should the stock go up, could grow without limit, but, of course, in the real world they would be capped.

Naked Puts

One of the most popular ways to sell options for income streams is to sell *naked puts.* There are some risks in this strategy, and you have to have a higher-level designation from your brokerage.

First, let's review what a put option entail. A put option gives the buyer the right, should they choose to exercise it, to sell 100 shares of the underlying stock at the strike price. They would use this strategy to make profits if the share price were to tank.

Consider an example. If the strike price of a put option was $50, and the share price dropped to $25, they could purchase the shares for $25 on the market, and then sell them to the writer of the put option at $50 a share. That would earn a $25 profit per share for the buyer. The only hope for the seller of the option is that the stock price rises again to make up the difference so that they can exit the position. Otherwise, they will suffer a huge loss.

However, there are strategies to protect yourself. When you sell options, you have the right to buy them back. So, if you sell a naked put and the stock starts tanking, you can limit your losses by buying them back.

Let's take a specific example. The share price is trading at $100 a share, and you write a naked put with a strike price of $103 with a 30-day expiry. The put is $5.17, so you earn a premium of $517. Let's say at 20 days to expiration, the price of the stock drops to $60 a share. The put option could be exercised, meaning that the option contract owner could buy the shares at $60, while you would be forced to buy them at the strike price, which was $103 a share. This is another example of big losses.

But you could have used a stop-loss order to mitigate your losses. Use the share price to determine your stop-loss order. We could use $95 as an example and suppose the declining stock hit this price with 24 days to expiration. In that case, the option would be $8.56, so we would be losing $3.39 a share. Buying back the options means that we don't have to buy the shares of stock. The $3.39 (per share) loss we have from buying back the options is painful to be sure, but it is still a lot better than having to come up with the money to buy 100 shares at $103 a share when they are only worth $60 a share on the market.

Please note that to sell naked options you must have a margin account, one with enough cash to cover the option as determined by a formula your broker uses. It depends on the price of the stock and the difference between the strike price and the share price. The amount, obviously, is way lower than what you would need to actually cover for the entire option.

Times when naked strategies could work

If the stock price is dropping it is the right time to write naked calls. In a market where stock prices are dropping, the odds are high that any call options written against the stock are going to expire worthlessly. Your profits from the premiums will be smaller, but the risk is also lower.

If the stock price is rising, instead, it is the right opportunity to write naked puts. The risk of the options being exercised in that case is reduced since it's far less likely that the share amount will go below the strike amount.

Besides, options sold out of the money always succeed in raising income without much risk. The trick is selling them far enough out of the money so that your risk is low. This strategy is routinely used by options traders to earn money via naked puts. If the share price starts getting close to your strike price you buy the option back to avoid getting assigned.

Chapter 2. Before You Enter a Trade

Let me stop you right there before you start making trades. There are a few things you need to be aware of before you enter the market. Let's read about them in this chapter so you can understand how to filter out the garbage and consistently pick good trades. Here are the steps you need to go through.

1. Portfolio Balance

Before you do anything, you need to look at your portfolio balance first. When you're planning a new trade, it's always important to ask yourself why you need that trade and how it will affect your portfolio. Do you even really need it? For instance, if your portfolio already has plenty of bearish trades, it would generally be better for you to avoid adding more.

You need to reduce your risk in every situation, so the key here is to balance out your trades. That's how one develops a great portfolio, risk diversification. When you have a bunch of bearish trades in hand, look for bullish trades to offset the risk and vice versa. Once you internalize this, it becomes far easier to focus on what your portfolio really needs and filter out the rest from the very first moment you start looking for a new trade.

2. Liquidity

Liquidity is straight up one of the most important qualities of a good, tradable option. You don't want to be stuck with an illiquid option, no matter how lucrative it looks. Here's a simple rule to follow when looking for a new trade: for it to be a good trade, the underlying stock should be trading at least 100,000 shares daily. If the numbers are less than that, the trade isn't worth your time. In a market as big and efficient as the one we have, the calculations only become more accurate with the passage of time. Similarly, when considering the underlying options, there should be a minimum of 1000 open interest contracts for the strikes you are trading for it to be a good trade. It ensures quick entry into and exit from the market. Remember, liquidity is important!

3. Implied Volatility Percentile

When a trade satisfies the previous two criteria, it's time to move on to the next step - the IV percentile. You need to check relatively how high or low the implied volatility of an option is, and this is measured by using percentile scores. Let me explain with an example.

Say, if AAPL has IV of 35% but IV percentile of 70%, it means that while the current volatility is low, in the last one year, it was higher than what it currently is (35%) for more than 70% of the time. So the implied volatility for AAPL is **relatively high**, and you should be looking to employ **premium-selling strategies**.

4. Picking a Strategy

Picking a great strategy is as much a matter of eliminating as it is a matter of selecting, perhaps even more so. You can easily eliminate a bunch of strategies once you have a good idea of the IV and the IV percentile of the underlying stock and how it affects the options. For example, it's easy to eliminate strategies like debit spreads and long single options when you know the IV is high and the pricing rich. Then it's time to consider our risk tolerance and account size to pick the best strategy out of the ones left (iron condors, credit spreads, strangles, etc.).

5. Strikes & Month

Your personal trading style and goals also play a big part in how you decide to pick trades. Some people are more risk-averse than others, and that's okay. You should always select the right strategy based on the risk level you're comfortable with. If you're selling credit spreads, let's say, and you have the option to sell them at either a strike price that has a 90% chance of success of a strike price that has a 65% chance of success, you need to decide which option you want to go with based on the level of aggression you're comfortable with. It needs to fit your trading style and your goals. Another thing that you need to do is give yourself sufficient time. This makes sure the trade can work out. This means that you should place low IV strategies at 60 to 90 days out and high IV strategies at 30 to 60 days out. To understand why this is the case, you should read up on Theta value (one of the Greeks) and how it affects volatility.

6. Position Size

Position sizing is one of those areas where even some of the more experienced traders fail. It's crucial that you understand this concept so you can make great trades often. Before placing a trade, you should always carefully assess your position size. As your trading position gets bigger, so does the risk, but this isn't linear, as many studies have shown. The risk increases exponentially, and one bad trade could easily lead to a blown account in this case. I strongly advise you to start with small positions as a beginner and continue to do so even when you're an intermediate. Your risk scale should be a sliding scale of 1 to 5% of your total balance on which all your trades need to be placed.

Now, how does one define this risk? Let me explain.

The cash or margin you use to cover a trade is what we call risk. For example, when selling a $1 wide credit put spread for 50 cents, you would need to cover it up with $50 margin. You use this $50 margin to base your trade off of for each trade you make. If your account is worth $20,000 and you wish to allocate 3% of your account (it fits the 1-5% sliding scale criteria), you can take $600 of risk (3% of $20,000). Then you divide this by $50 and you get 12, which is the number of spreads you should sell at most. If this number is a fraction, always round down and never up.

7. Future Moves

You must've heard the popular saying that a chess grandmaster can foresee as many as 20 moves ahead. A good options trader also plans ahead and foresees future moves. If you're not thinking a few moves ahead, you're going to lose to the market more often than not. Always have a Plan B in case things go nasty and you need to shield yourself from losses. And while shielding yourself from a losing trade is important, it's also important to plan how to turn a losing situation into a winning one.

Sometimes, you just won't be able to make a winning trade. That's just how the market works; some trades go wrong no matter how well you plan. But you need to keep asking yourself the important questions constantly. When you do this, your mind stays sharp and ready to jump into action to formulate a new plan or make an adjustment as and when the need arises.

Chapter 3.   Creating   Your   Own Day Trading Strategy

As you start to get more into day trading, you may decide to develop your own strategy. There are a lot of great trading strategies that are out there. There may be some market conditions or other situations where you need to be able to develop your own strategy. Or, after trying out a few different things, you end up finding a new strategy, or a combination of strategies, that ends up working out the best.

Over time, it is important that you find your own place inside the market. As you go through, you may even find that you would rather be more like a swing trader rather than a day trader just because of the different methods that are available. The good news is, there is a market for any kind of trader, and there are a million types of strategies that you can use based on your own personal preferences along the way.

Before you jump into the market as a beginner with your own trading strategy, it is important that you start out by picking one of the strategies that are in this guidebook (or another proven strategy that you have researched). You need to have some time to try out a strategy and tread through the market a bit before you start coming up with your own strategy. Even if you have invested in the stock market before, you will find that working with day trading is completely different compared to some of the other methods available, and you do not want to pick a strategy that may have worked with one of your other trades, but will make you fail miserably with day trading.

It is all about spending some time in the market and getting familiar with the market. You will want to get familiar with how the day trading market works, how to recognize good stocks and so on before you make a good strategy that can help you. After spending some time in the market, working with one or two strategies that you like, you will be able to learn the patterns that you like and what to watch out for, and it becomes so much easier to make a strategy that will actually work.

But no matter where you are as a trader, it is so important that every trader has a strategy of some sort to help them get started. It is so easy for beginners to just pick out a stock and then start trading, without having a plan in place at all. This is a dangerous thing to work with. It pretty much leaves the decisions up to your emotions, and we all know how dangerous this can be when you are first starting out. You should never leave your trades up to the emotions; this will make you stay in the market too long or leave the market too early, and you will end up losing money.

In addition, you need to pick one strategy, whether it is one from this guidebook or one that you made up on your own, and then you need to stick with that strategy. Learn all of the rules that go with that strategy, how to make that strategy work for you, and exactly how you should behave at different times in the market with that strategy. Even if it ends up leading you to a bad trade (remember that any type of strategy and even the best traders will end up with a bad trade on occasion), you will stick it out until the trade is done. You can always switch strategies in between trades, but it is never a good idea to switch your strategy once you are already in the market.

Switching strategies can seem tempting when you are a beginner in the market. You may see that things are going south or may realize once you are in the market that you should have done a different strategy from the beginning. But as you look through some of the strategies that are in this guidebook, you probably notice that they are a bit different, and they need some different requirements before you can get in and out of the trade. Switching in the middle is not going to work and will lead to an automatic loss.

The most important thing that you can remember when you become a day trader is that all traders will fail at some point. Many beginners will fail because they do not take the time to learn how to properly day trade or they let their emotions get in the way of making smart decisions. But even advanced traders will have times when they will fail and lose money as well. The market is not always the most reliable thing in the world. Even when you are used to reading the charts and looking at the market, there will be times when it does not act as expected and a trader will lose out. Or the advanced trader may choose to try out a new strategy, and it does not work that well for them.

There will be times when you will lose money, and this can be hard to handle for a lot of beginners. This is also why you need to consider how much you can actually afford to lose on a trade before you enter the market. You do not want to go all out on your first trade because it is likely you will fail and lose that money or maybe more depending on the trade.

If you are worried about getting started in the market or you want to mess around and try out a few of the strategies ahead of time to see how they work, especially if you are using one of your own strategies, then you should consider working with a simulator. Sometimes you will be able to get one of these from your broker to try out and experiment with the market, and sometimes you may have to pay a bit from another site to use this simulator. However, this can be a valuable tool that will help you to try out different things, make changes, and get a little familiarity in the market before you invest your actual money. As a beginner, if you have access to one of these simulators, it is definitely worth your time to give it a try.

Picking your trade based on the time of day

Before we move on, we will take a look at which types of strategies seem to work the best at different times of the day. As you get into the market, you will notice that each time period of the day will be different and there are some patterns that seem to show up over time with them. We will work with three times of day, the open, the mid-day, and the close. If you want to be successful with day trading, it is not a good idea to use the same strategy at all three times of the day because these strategies will not be successful at all times of the day. The best traders will figure out what time of day they get the most profitable trades and then they will make some adjustments to their strategies and their trading to fit them into these profitable times.

First, let's talk about the open. This time period will last about an hour and a half, starting at 9:30 in the morning on New York Time. This is a busy time of the day because people are joining the market for the first time or they are making adjustments based on how their stocks had done overnight. Because this time is so busy, it can also be a really profitable time period if you play the game right. It is a good idea to increase the size of your trades during this time and do more of them because you are more likely to make some good money during this time. The best strategies to use during the open will be the VWAP trades and the Bull Flag Momentum.

Next session is the mid-day session, and this will start at 11 in the morning and go for about four hours. This is a slow time in the market, and it is considered one of the more dangerous times to trade during the day. There is not going to be much liquidity or volume in the market. Even a smaller order will make a stock move quite a bit during this time, so you really need to watch the market if you are holding onto your stocks. It is more likely that you will be stopped with unexpected and strange moves during this period.

It is common for many traders, both beginners and those who are more advanced, to have a lot of trouble during the mid-day. Many decide that it is not the best idea to work in the market during this time. But if you do decide to trade, it is important to keep the stops tight and also to lower your share size. You should also be really picky about the risk and reward ratio during this time. You will find that new traders will often do their overtrading during this time, and it may be best to simply avoid trading during this time period altogether.

If you do decide to trade during the mid-day, it is best to watch the stocks as closely as possible, get some things ready for close, and always be very careful about any trading decisions that you try to do. You will find that support or resistance trades, moving average, VWAP, and reversal strategies work well during the mid-day.

And finally, there is the close, which starts at 3 in the afternoon and goes for about an hour. These stocks are considered more directional, so it is best to stick with those that are going either down or up during this last hour. It is possible to raise the tier size compared to what it was at in mid-day, but you do not want to go as high as you were at open. You will find that the prices at closing are often going to reflect what the traders on Wall Street think the value of the stocks is. These traders have stayed out of the market during the day, but they have been closely watching things so that they can get in and dominate what happens during the last little bit of trading.

It is also common to see that many market professionals will sell their stocks at this time and take the profits because they do not want to hold onto the trades overnight. As a day trader, you will be one of these professionals because you need to sell all of your stocks on the same day to be a day trader.

If you notice that the stock starts to move higher during this last hour, this means that the professionals are considered bullish on that stock. However, if you see that the stock starts to move lower in that last hour, it means that the professionals in the market are considered bearish. It is best during this last hour to work with trades that go with these professionals, rather than doing trades that go against them. When you decide to trade in the closing hour, you will want to use the moving average trades, support and resistance trades, or VWAP to get the best results.

As a beginner trader, you may find that you will profit during the open and then end up with a lot of losses during the rest of the day. A good rule of thumb that you can stick with to keep things conservative with your losses is that you should never lose more than 30 percent of what you made in the open during the rest of the day. If you reach that 30 percent, you will stop trading for the day to protect your assets.

Chapter 4. Candlestick Common Patterns

When it comes to analyzing traded assets such as futures, bonds, stocks and so on, a normally seen pattern on the candlestick is the doji.

Doji

When you see it, you will notice that it has a length that is minute. What this means is that there a minute trading range, with the closing and opening price being equal.

The doji is meant to show the level of indecision that is found in the market. If the market, at the moment, isn't trending properly, the doji won't be significant at that movement. This is because these markets that are not trending show high level of indecision.

If you notice that the doji has either a downtrend or uptrend, what this means is that buyers are currently losing conviction if it is seen in an uptrend format. If it is noticed in the downward format, that means that the sellers are currently losing conviction.

Types of Doji

1. Neutral Doji

This type of doji forms when it is noticeable that both the closing and open prices are both equal. Normally, dojis without interference have neutral pattern.

2. Long legged Doji

This is a reflection of a high amount of indecision that one faces concerning where the underlying asset is going in the future.

3. Gravestone Doji

If you see a long upper shadow, this means that the trend's direction may be getting close to the main turning point.

This occurs when you notice that the underlying asset's closing and opening price are equal, while happening at the lowest part of the day.

4. Dragonfly Doji

When you notice the long lower shadow, it means that the trend's direction may be getting close to the main turning point. You will see it when the asset's closing and opening price are similar. This happens typically in the highest part of the day.

The doji acts as the major trend reversal indicator. This situation usually is true when you noticed a large amount of trade, which is following a heightened movement in any direction.

When you notice the following you should know that there is a great chance that a downtrend will occur within the few next days. If the market has seen as an uptrend, thereby trading using a higher high than what was seen in the prior days, and if the high doesn't hold, thereby closing in the lower ten percent of the trading range of the day, then this will occur, and vice versa.

As a horizontal line, the 4-Price Doji line shows that the close, open, low and high are equal.

Tweezers

Tweezers came into existence when Steve Nison, the person that popularized candlestick charting in the West region, showed the pattern in "Japanese Candlestick Charting Techniques."

You can see tweezers in different forms, but they have a number of similar characteristics.

They sometimes show at the market-turning points, and they can be utilized in running analysis. This is meant to show if there is a probability of reversal occurring.

They are also utilized broadly when trend traders want to see trade signals.

Before the candlesticks came to the West, the Japanese have utilized this for long centuries. They make use of them when they want to trade things. This started from the 17th century, thereby making the charts a lot popular. When it comes to monitoring the price data, these charts are the perfect ways of doing such.

A candle's body is normally formed by the disparity that exists between the close and open. Those thin shadows that you see on the different part of the candle show the low and high during that period.

The red or dark candle translates to the open that was above the close. The green or white candle means that the price ended above how it opened.

It indicates a shift in trend

The tweezers are meant to act as the bottoming and topping patterns. This pattern ends up showing the change in the direction of the trend. It is also used to confirm if the signal is true because the tweezers tend to happen a lot.

You will see a topping pattern if the two candlesticks' highs happen close to similar level tailing the advancement.

The bottoming pattern happens when the two candlesticks' lows happen close to a similar level when a decline happens.

An extra set of criteria involve the first candle possessing a real big body, while the second one can have any size. This means that both candles may sometimes look differently.

Let's use an example. The top of the tweezers may have a first candlestick that is very strong, ending close to the high. On the other hand, the second candle may take the form of a doji that won't end close to the high but may possess the same high seen in the first candle.

Importance of the pattern

The tweezer is known to look like a different reversal candlestick pattern, and this is important. Examples of topping patterns are dark cloud cover and bearish engulfing pattern. The bottom pattern that you should consider watching is a piercing pattern and a bullish engulfing pattern.

These candlesticks do not look like tweezers every time, but whenever they take the form of tweezers, they input some significance to the pattern.

Usually, special tweezers patterns tend to display a substantial alteration in the momentum from a day to the next one.

If you notice a strong up bar tailing a shooting start candle or a hanging man candle, then you should not assume that it is a significant reversal pattern. This is true especially when the price ends beneath the real body of the second candle inside the other couple of candles.

The bottoming pattern is usually the strong down candle that is tailed by the hammer.

A short-term bottom is usually former when a close appear on top of the hammer body

Candlestick patterns, in most cases, happen, and the same can be said for tweezers. Whether they are significant or not is dependent on their look.

If you notice a general trend while the tweezers happen in a pullback, it shows that this is a prospective entry point. It shows that the pullback gas ended, and there is a great chance that the price may swing to the trending direction once more.

When you make use of tweezers like this, the pattern's success rate tends to be heightened.

In a bottom pattern, you will notice that stop loss is put beneath the lows of the tweezers.

In a topping pattern, you will notice that the stop loss is put on the highs of the tweezers. It is important to note that the tweezers do not give a profit target, meaning that you should base the target on a number of factors like overall momentum and trend.

Morning Star

This is a visual pattern that shows three candlesticks that end up being a bullish sign to technical analysts. The morning start is formed by following the downward trend, while showing the beginning of an upward climb. This is a symbol that there was a reversal in the prior price trend.

When traders see morning star forming, they go ahead to see if there is any confirmation that a reversal in trend is occurring. They do this by making use of extra indicators.

Since it is only a visual pattern, you don't have to do any calculations. The morning star usually begins after three sessions. If it doesn't come then, it is not coming. You can use technical indicators to see if a morning star will form anytime in the future.

Differences between a Doji morning star and a morning star.
Sometimes, the morning star pattern may have a minute disparity. If the price action ends up being flat in the middle candlestick, it becomes a doji. When you see a tiny candlestick and no major wicks, then it is a doji. The Doji morning star is a reflection of the high level of market indecision, which the morning star doesn't show well even after having a thicker middle candle

When a doji follows a black candle, it usually leads to a highly aggressive volume spike than a longer white candle.

Difference Between Evening and Morning Stars.

The morning star and the evening star are quite opposite to one another. You can spot an evening star when you spot a long white candle that is followed by a darker one that is short. After that, the long black one reduces to about half of the white candle during the initial session.

When you see the evening star, know that an uptrend is about to be reversed, meaning that the bulls are retiring for the bears.

When you trade only on visual patterns, it is very risky.

Using a morning star is great when you back it up by both volume and an indicator such as a support level.

Chapter 5.   Call Spreads

Spread strategies are more advanced in that you don't need to establish a long position. Thus, the cost of establishing a position is a lot lower than with the covered call or the collar trade. While your long-term options trading base should be rooted in those strategies, pursuing spread trades will give you healthy returns in the short term.

Spread trades work very much in principle like collar trades except you will be buying and selling calls (or puts) of the same month and the same type of option in every trade. In other words, while you were selling calls and buying puts with the collar, in this case, you will be buying and selling calls or buying and selling puts.

Bull Call Spreads

One of the biggest benefits of trading options is that you don't need to be terribly worried about the current market situation since your trades are designed to profit in all markets. At the very least, you will have a strategy, no matter what the market is doing. The bull call spread, also called the long call spread, is a strategy for a moderate to strong bullish market.

In this scenario, you're quite certain that the stock is going to increase in value over the medium term but you're a bit uncertain about the volatility it is showing. You see, there is a dose of uncertainty with every directional position and you are compensated for this with higher rewards. Options strategies take this uncertainty away but cap your maximum reward.

Thus, if you're extremely certain that a stock is going to go upwards for sure, buying a long call is probably the best strategy. After all, if you know a stock is going to increase in value, why would you place a cap on your profits by writing a call at a higher strike price?

Such situations are extremely rare; however, and this is where the bull call spread comes into action.

How it Works

With the bull call spread, you will be buying a long call which is either in the money or close to the money and offsetting this price by writing an out of the money call. If the stock goes past the higher strike price, your long call is in profit but your overall profit is capped to the level of the higher strike price.

If the stock goes below your long call, you have the premium of the higher strike price call to offset your loss, which is simply the premium you paid for the long call. Remember, you're not buying any stock in this strategy so there is no loss on the stock itself.

Let's continue to use AAPL as an example of this. As of this writing, AAPL is trading at $173.3. The closest at the money call option in the near month is the $170 and $175 which is trading at $6.95 and $4.10 respectively. Now, you could choose either of these strike prices. Remember, you're moderately bullish on the stock but are not sure how high it will go. Given these conditions, let's purchase the 175 call for $4.10.

Now, we need to find a suitable strike price to write a call at. This is a tricky balancing act. Write a call too far away and you won't receive enough of a premium. Write one too close, and you're not giving your trade enough breathing room. This is why it's essential to keep your time horizon on this trade as short as you can afford to. Ideally, your options will have some time value left on them but not too much time so as to bring price uncertainty into them.

The time decay is evident in the current month option prices. The $190 option is selling for $0.37 which is a pittance really. However, let's stick with the current month for now. So what do our risk and reward look like?

Maximum risk= Premium paid for long call- Premium received for short call= 4.1-0.37= 3.73.

Maximum reward= Strike price of short call- Strike price of long call- cost paid for entering the trade= 190-175-3.73= 11.27

Thus our reward/risk on this 3X. Just to clarify, the prices quoted for an option contract are on a per share basis. Since every contract contains a hundred shares, you should multiply the price by a hundred to get the full price of the contract.

So, to enter this position, or to purchase a single contract, we will need to spend $373 and if the price hits our higher strike price of $190 then we'll clear $1127 on the trade. These numbers are with the near month options, of course. Let's look at how the numbers change by taking the far month into consideration.

Price of far month $175 call= $6.30

Price of far month $190 call= $0.92

Cost of entering the trade and maximum risk/share= 6.3-.92=5.38

Maximum profit/share= 15-5.38= 9.62

This gives us a reward risk of $1.78, which isn't all that great, to be honest. As you can see the vagaries of option pricing affect the profit and loss calculations quite a bit. In this case, due to the existing sentiment on AAPL, perhaps the far month calls are priced lower than the near month.

I've assumed a bullish condition but this is not reflected in the prices as you can see. In reality, the far month prices, in a bullish trend, will have higher prices and it is worthwhile for you to check them out as well if you're confident of the trend in the near term.

Considerations

Given the lack of a long stock position, your margin up front is a lot less on the bull call spread. Also, since the risk is defined by the premium you pay up front, figuring out the number of contracts you wish to carry is pretty straight forward. Simply figure out how much percent of your account the max risk is and make sure it is a low enough number that won't hit your account too hard in case the trade goes south.

Of course, bullish conditions are the primary underlying factor in the trade. If the market is wildly bullish, then there's no point in executing this since you'll only be limiting your gains. However, a volatile market, which is seeing a lot of counter-trend activity, provides an excellent set of conditions for you to deploy this strategy in.

Use technical indicators to determine the short-term direction and deploy this strategy wisely.

Bear Call Spreads

Bear or short call spreads are a trade which have an inverted reward risk profile but an extremely high success rate, assuming everything is executed well. This is a strategy that a lot of professional's love, thanks to it being a steady income earner. However, risk management is absolutely critical since the potential loss you could incur is many multiples of the amount of money you stand to make.

This is a strategy where money keeps flowing in with small wins but execute something wrong and one loss will wipe everything away. A lot of beginners experience this due to getting complacent after the steady stream of money coming in.

This strategy is for sideways markets which are at a resistance zone or bearish markets. While selling a call is the best way to take advantage of a bear market, it is unlikely your broker will allow you to do this right off the bat. Hence, the bear call spread is an excellent strategy to deploy in such times.

How it Works

With a bear call spread, you will be writing an at the money or slightly out of the money call and buying a well out of the money option. Thus, on entering the trade, you will receive the premium from the lower strike price call and pay the lesser premium of the higher strike price call.

This is also the amount of your maximum profit on the trade. If the underlying stock increases in price beyond the first call, you will need to exercise your higher strike price call to buy the shares to fulfill the lower call being exercised. Thus, it is vital that your strike prices are close together and not too far apart, or else your trade will be stuck in a no man's land.

All of this is better illustrated via an example. AAPL is currently trading at $173.30 and the closest at the money call is $175, priced at $4.75. Now, let's assume $175 is a major resistance and that the stock is certain to turn back downwards once it reaches here. We write a call at $175 and earn the $4.75 premium.

It is a good idea to buy calls which are two steps past the lower strike price level. At this point in time, the strike price that is two steps away is the $180 call, which can be bought for $2.84.

Cost of trade entry/maximum profit per share= Premium received from writing lower call- Premium paid to purchase higher call= 4.75- 2.84= $1.91/ share.

Maximum loss= Strike price of higher call- strike price of lower call-net premium received on trade entry= 180-175-1.91= $3.09/share.

As you can see, the reward risk is inverted with this strategy. Now, the best-case scenario for this trade is for both options to expire out of the money. In that case, you don't need to bother exercising either one of them.

The no man's land scenario is if the lower call moves into the money but the higher call doesn't. In this case, you'll have to buy the shares yourself, physically, at whatever the market price is and deliver the shares thanks to the lower call being exercised.

The worst-case scenario is price moving past the higher call, in which case you'll need to exercise it and deliver it. You'll obviously eat the entire loss in this case. This is why it is very important to make sure the price is in a strong bear trend or is near a strong resistance from which it will turn downwards.

Given the risk of this strategy, I personally recommend beginners to stick to options which are in the current month, instead of trying to capture the time decay of near month options. The additional time risk is too much and most beginners will not be able to manage risk well enough to stomach such losses.

Considerations

Your biggest concern with the bear call spread is the risk. Sure, you could widen the gap between the lower and higher call but to do so, you must be completely certain that the probability of price rising beyond the lower call is low. As always, market conditions play a huge role and you must be aware of these at all times.

What if you happen to be wrong about your market premise? What if, instead of being bearish, it turns out that the market makes a bull move? Well, this is where the adjustment comes into play.

You could flip your bear spread into a bull spread or, in the case of an expected bull market turning bearish, you could turn a bull spread into a bearish one. As always, the call levels are important. Needless to say, you need to buy and sell the same number of contracts and both legs of the trade must belong to the same calendar month.

Don't get fancy and try to arbitrage different months or make a volatility play. If you don't know what that sentence meant then don't worry. It was aimed at those traders who know just enough to trip themselves up.

Stick to the basics of these strategies and you'll find yourself making money consistently. If you are wondering if it's possible to successfully leverage calls with different month expiry dates, then yes, it is possible. This is what the calendar spread trade is all about.

Open Positions & Contracts

In this section, we are going to explore how forex contracts are priced and executed, first by considering some of the broad concepts, and then move on to some simple examples which I hope will show you how it all works.

As soon as you open a position on a currency pair, four things happen simultaneously.

First, you have used some of your initial margin to support this position, so the amount of your initial margin remaining has fallen.

Second, your broker has loaned you some money to fund the position.

Third, the position is now moving between profit and loss second by second

Finally, whilst your balance has remained unchanged, your overall equity position has changed, and before moving on let me just explain the difference between balance and equity as they are not the same thing. The balance in the account is the physical cash balance, so just like a bank statement it reflects how much cash you have in the account at the time.

When you first open your account, and deposit say $1,000, then your balance will say $1,000.

Equity on the other hand reflects the live position of your account at any one time. Taking the same example, if we had an open position in the market which was $200 in profit, then your equity would be $1,200. This would change second by second, and I'll explain this in a moment.

Next, let's look at this from the broker's perspective. All brokers are in business to make a profit, and therefore profits have to be protected at all times, particularly in the volatile world of forex trading. How do they do this?

Well, whilst they are happy to lend you money against your initial margin, they will only do this up to a point, as they have no intention whatsoever of subsidizing any losses you may make with their money. In order to avoid this potential situation arising, every forex brokerage account has a trigger which sets the alarm bells ringing, and the mechanism used is called maintenance margin.

We're going to do a very simple example shortly, but before we do, let me just try to explain some of the broad concepts to lay the foundations for you.

First, as soon as you open a trading position then you have an unrealized P & L (profit and loss) on the account, which will change in real time, second by second, and this is unrealized.

In other words you haven't closed out the position or positions to take a profit or a loss, which will then be reflected in your account in both the balance and the equity.

If you have no open positions, then your balance and equity will be the same. In other words, the cash in the account. If you do have open positions, then the balance will reflect the cash amount in the account before you opened these positions, whilst the equity will reflect the balance plus any unrealized profits or losses.

In our example above, if we have a $200 profit in an open position the balance would read $1,000 and the equity would read $1,200, and if the position were closed at this point, then both the equity and the balance would be the same at $1,200.

Now, maintenance margin, as the name implies, is the margin that your broker requires to be in the account at all times in order for you to continue trading. If it falls to or below this level, then any positions you have open in the account will be closed in order to protect you, and more importantly your broker. Maintenance margin is also often referred to as variation margin, but essentially these are one and the same. Once again, this changes second by second, as soon as you have an open position in the market.

Finally, before we look at a simple example, let me just introduce two more terms here, which will make the example more realistic, and these are 'useable margin', and 'used margin' which work in a close relationship with our initial margin.

Let's assume once again that we have opened our account with our $1,000 and we have no open positions, so our useable margin is $1,000 as we haven't used any of this yet to support a market position, and the used margin is 0, since we haven't used any to open any positions.

However, as soon as we open a position then the useable margin will fall and the used margin will rise by the same amount. If we had used $100 in margin to support a position, then our usable margin would be $900, and our used margin would be $100.

Now let's look at a very simple example and we're going to ignore commissions and spreads as it's an unnecessary complication. We now have our four principle terms within our trading account, namely, balance, equity, useable margin and used margin.

The key relationship that your broker will be monitoring second by second, and so should you, is that between equity and used margin, and this is what creates the trigger for your broker, when the alarm bells will start ringing. And the trigger is this.

If the equity in your account is greater than the used margin, then your broker will be happy and your account is not in danger. If the equity in your account falls to, or below, the used margin, then this will trigger the alarm bell, and your broker will do one of two things. First, he or she will close out some or all of your positions to prevent any further loss. Second, they may or may not contact you for more funds, often known as a margin call, which simply means more cash is needed in the account - immediately. And if this is not received within the required time, which is normally hours, then your position or positions will be closed, in order to bring your equity level back above the used margin level once more.

In other words this is a very simple equation which is as follows:

Useable margin = Equity - Used Margin

For the broker this means that their money is never put at risk by your actions, and this in simple terms is really what margin is all about. It is your broker, 'locking away' portions of cash which are his protection in the event of things going wrong. Think of them as locked safes, where you broker has deposited some of your cash.

Let's take a simple example, and then we'll look at how the maintenance margin then fits in alongside, and once again, how this works will vary from broker to broker, so you will need to check this carefully.

Let's go back to our well-worn example, using our simple $1,000 once more:

- Balance - $1,000
- Equity - $1,000
- Useable margin - $1,000
- Used margin - $0

We then open a small position which requires $100 of margin. How does our account change?

- Balance - $1,000
- Equity - $1,000
- Useable margin - $900
- Used margin - $100

Sometime later, we check our account and find that our position has deteriorated, and we are now looking at a potential loss of $500. How does our account look now?

- Balance - $1,000
- Equity - $500
- Useable margin - $400
- Used margin - $100

Well, our balance is still the same at $1,000 as we haven't closed the position yet. Our equity is now $1,000 minus the potential loss of $500, so this is $500. Our usable margin is now $900 minus $500 so $400 (which is from our simple equation above), and our used margin remains unchanged at $100.

Now at this point our equity of $500 is still greater than our used margin at $100, so we have not reached our danger level yet in terms of the margin level required to continue trading with this position open. However, let's assume the situation gets worse. We check again, and now the position is $900 in loss. What does the account look like now?

- Balance - $1,000

- Equity - $100

- Useable margin - $100

- Used margin - $100

Well, our balance is still $1,000, our equity is now $1,000 minus $900 which is $100. Our useable margin is now $1,000 minus $900 which is $100, and our used margin is still $100. However, our equity is now equal to our used margin at $100 and the alarm bell will ring as we are about to break below the margin level required. Your broker will not allow this to happen as it means potentially that he could then be responsible for your losses, and his automated systems will trigger a margin call to you.

At this point, you either add further funds into the account, which will lift your balance and your equity, which in turn will then be higher than the used margin once more. Or your position will be closed by the broker, and your account will then look like this:

- Balance - $100
- Equity - $100
- Useable margin - $100
- Used margin - $0

The balance is now $100 as we have closed the position and taken the loss of -$900 into our account. Our equity is now also $100 as we have no open positions. The useable margin is now $100 and the margin used is back to zero, as we have no open positions in our account.

My golden rule is this. If you ever receive a margin call then your trading is out of control, and you should stop immediately. It's as simple as that - sorry! You should never, ever receive a margin call if you are running your trading account correctly, which you will be, once you have finished reading this book!

In the last example, we assumed that the broker would issue a margin call at the precise point at which the equity was equal to the used margin, but this is not always the case. Some brokers will offer you the option to use a percentage of this 'used margin' to support further losses. You can think of this as though the broker has locked this money away for your own protection, but allows you to have some back 'if required', and this brings in the concept of 'maintenance margin' which may be below the 'used margin'.

Suppose for example, that your broker has a policy whereby their maintenance margin level is 50% of the used margin, then in this case you would have a further $50 of margin to use to support the position. Here, you would receive a margin call at this lower level, when the position was a further $50 in loss. If closed at this level, then your account would look like this:

- Balance - $50

- Equity - $50

- Useable margin - $50

- Used margin - $0

Every broker account will be different in terms of the words they use and the layout of the account. You may come across slightly different terms such as free margin, or available margin, as well as required margin and variation margin along with maintenance margin. However, the fundamental principle of how margin works remain the same.

Again, you can think of this as a safety measure taken by your broker who is locking money away to protect himself. After all, unexpected events can happen at the weekend when the markets are closed, including natural disasters, shock economic events, and world events, all of which can impact the forex market. It is not surprising that your broker will allow for such events in the margin calculations. The same applies to positions held overnight.

But the key point is this. Provided you understand how the account is constructed in terms of the underlying margin requirements, you should never have to worry about approaching any of the trigger levels, provided you follow the rules and trading methods I explain here. I will be covering risk and money management later, so please don't worry. All you need is here, and I hope explained both simply and clearly.

I also hope that wasn't too confusing and you now understand the basic concepts of margin. It's so important. Please just take time to go over these examples again if you are a little confused. It is actually relatively simple once you can get your head round the idea of the broker not wanting to lose any money, which is really all it's about at the end of the day.

Chapter 6. Strategy for Selling Covered Calls

There's a whole list of considerations that you will eventually want to bear in mind as you expand your knowledge and develop your own, personal strategy. Every trader has a different attitude towards what works and what doesn't – there are plenty of ways to make selling a covered call work, but you'll probably find yourself preferring one or two strategies.

We'll take a look now at those considerations in more detail to guide you as you delve into the covered call more deeply:

The Market Environment: You are no doubt aware that traders of stocks and shares are happy in a bull market and disgruntled in a bear market. You may also know that such traders hate a flat market most of all, because very little is happening and there aren't many big profits to be made. For you, as a seller of covered calls, the opposite is true. I highly recommend

[handwritten marginalia: "Side Way Market Best For Covered Calls"]

waiting for the market to temporarily flatten before embarking on a spate of covered call sales. This is because you're only really interested in small changes to your share prices – if they are skyrocketing, you're losing more money on your contract. There also isn't as much danger of the bottom falling out of the market and your stock prices plummeting at the same time, which would be problematic.

• *Your Underlying Stock:* There is nothing more important to your success than choosing the right stocks to invest in in the first place. I cannot stress strongly enough that your success will be heightened if you pick stocks that move up very slowly. You don't want stocks that rise and fall very quickly, especially as a beginner, because they have a habit of making surprising moves that ruin your strategy. If they drop too far, you stand to lose a lot of money in the sale; if they rise too high, you lose the money you could have made if you'd sold them at that price. Traders who deal in risk often enjoy these stocks because they have higher premiums and a chance for huge profits, but that goes against the idea of selling covered calls: you're looking for a steady income that will underpin your riskier strategies elsewhere. By all means go for the riskier stock elsewhere in your strategy, but avoid it like the plague for this particular function.

• *The Premium:* Always remember that the premium is your guaranteed profit. Whatever else happens, you're going to walk away with that cash. When you factor in the cost to list the option and any commission you will lose to your broker, you'll be able to calculate the actual profit you'll make on that premium. Set yourself a minimum premium – a number that you consider to be enough to provide a profit you'll be happy with, on the assumption that it's the only profit you make. When you move ahead on setting the strike price, you'll likely adjust this base figure up or down based on what you think the underlying stock is going to do before the expiration date. Remember that the premium is only one component of the overall profit you will make – if you then set a strike price that means you lose the same amount of cash on selling the shares as you made through the premium, the trade wasn't worth doing in the first place.

• *The Expiration Date:* There's a reason that the premiums on covered calls get higher the further out the expiration date. It's because, much like the weather forecasts we all deride on a daily basis, it gets harder and harder to predict what's going to happen to a share price the further out you go. Also bear in mind that your money is going to be tied up until the expiration date, so the premium will increase as a nod to that sacrifice. Most investors believe that a time span of between a month and three months works best. *BeTWeeN A MONTh & 3 MO.*

• *The Strike Price:* You might think that the strike price you set should be based on what you, as the seller, are comfortable with, but actually it's the opposite. You're looking for a strike price that your buyer will feel comfortable with, because otherwise they aren't going to buy. That, in turn, is going to be dictated by the expiration date you set, as well as the premium you're asking for and how stable or volatile the underlying stock is. Your best bet is to put yourself in the shoes of your buyer: would you purchase that contract? How much would you stand to gain? Set your strike price accordingly and then take a look at it from your own point of view. Would this be an acceptable profit for you? If so, you've hit the nail on the head.

With all these factors in mind, you are likely starting to see that there is no single "correct decision" when it comes to selling covered calls. It's going to take practice and concentration to figure out which ones work best for you.

It's also important to note that your strategy is probably going to change as you gain experience. The more options you sell, the more you will see new and more advanced ways to take advantage of the market. For now, I urge you to be conservative in your approach and accept that selling covered options is not going to win you your fortune – but it is going to help you increase the seed money you have available to do just that.

Outcomes of a Covered Sell

As we're using the idea of selling covered calls as a trade example to help you learn the basics of option trading overall, let's now take a close look at what is going to happen to your option once you've listed it.

> • *The stock increases in value:* If the stock moves up and hits your strike price, this means that your buyer can now exercise their right and buy the shares. The more it rises, the more likely that the buyer will do exactly that. When your goal is to sell shares, this is what you want to happen – and you will pocket the premium as well as, of course, the difference between the shares as they were valued when you listed them and the value they are at on the expiration date (in other words, capital gains).

> • *The stock value doesn't move:* If the shares don't change either up or down during the time the option is open, then they

won't hit the strike price and you won't have to sell. You will pocket the premium and can factor it into your overall profits when you relist the stock. Many options traders actually count on this outcome – it's the one they are hoping for because it means they make a profit AND keep the shares. Feel free to follow the same logic, but make sure your entire plan doesn't hinge on it. You don't control the market, so you could find yourself met by a nasty surprise.

- *The stock drops in value:* If this happens, the outcome is very similar to the share price not moving at all. The difference is that you are losing money on the shares themselves all the time they are dropping. They might bounce back, but if they don't then the expiration date will arrive and you'll be holding shares that are now worth a lot less than they used to be, which constitutes a loss. If, while monitoring your option contracts, you see that a stock is starting to drop, you need to prepare to take emergency action. Do this by calculating your "breakeven" price: subtract the premium per share from the price of the share at the time you listed it. For example, if the share was worth $50 and the premium per share is $1.50, your breakeven price per share is $48.50. If it falls below this price, you have the option to buy back your option – not something you should rely on or do often, but good as an emergency action. To do this, go back to the order entry and select "Buy to Close". Enter either the current ask price or something lower, depending how risky you want to be. Once the trade goes through, you are back in control of your shares and can either keep or sell them, as you deem fit.

As an aside, you should know that buying back your options is actually a deliberate strategy used by some people who trade in covered calls. Doing so allows you to manage your own risk, ending trades that are likely to be disadvantageous for you so that you can list those stocks again at a later date.

For instance, let's say that your underlying stock is rising fast and you think you're going to lose out on a lot of potential profit as it continues to skyrocket. You could "roll up" your options by buying back your call at the current ask price or lower and then selling them again at a higher strike price.

Simply setting your stock to sell is enough to garner you a regular income to support your options trading, but there are other ways you can make the most of the market.

Buy
+ Sell
A Call
at Same
Time

A typical strategy for a person who deals in selling covered calls is to purchase a stock and sell a covered call on that stock at the exact same time. It's called a "Buy-Write Strategy". Your brokerage firm will almost certainly allow you to do this and may even have it listed on their online order screen for you to select.

So what would you be looking for if you did this?

- A stock that you would be happy to have in your share portfolio, assuming that the buyer never realized their right to purchase it.

- A stock that is showing a premium rate on the marketplace you would be happy to accept.

- A stock that is predictable in that it is rising or dipping in worth slowly over time.

Keep your eyes firmly on the stock market over time and you will start to see those trends. You'll also develop an eye for spotting good trades – the ones where you can make a quick profit by selling a few contracts at a good premium price.

A second advanced strategy is to use options trading to get rid of stocks you don't want to own any more. Maybe, for instance, they've been flat for a long time and you aren't seeing enough movement to make them worthwhile. You can set up a sell that would return a good premium while allowing you to get rid of your stocks at close to their current price. Instead of simply unloading them, you'd walk away with the premium as a potentially tidy profit.

Thirdly, you can choose to use the "half and half" strategy: keep some of your stocks in a particular company and sell the rest. This works well if you aren't really sure whether you should sell them all, but make sure you are keeping records of what you have done.

Stepping Up a Tier: Buying Calls

We're ready to move on to the more sophisticated areas of options trading. You have tested the waters, made a little cash and you feel comfortable with the mechanics of the market. Now, you can start actually buying those calls and hopefully begin to make some real money as you do.

It's actually a simpler business to buy a call, in terms of physically going ahead and doing so. However, it's not quite so easy to make a profit. You're going to need to start small and dedicate yourself to the learning curve – and you need to understand that there is a risk involved in buying calls, so you don't want to stake your life savings on your efforts.

Let me take the opportunity to advise you to build up slowly over time rather than jump straight in with a hundred buys in a single day. Be circumspect about your actions: a small profit is better than no profit at all. Save your riskiest ideas for when you've set up a nest egg through your sells and you feel confident enough in your own judgment that you're as sure as it's possible to be that your risk will pay off.

As a reminder, what you are actually doing when you buy a call is purchasing the right to buy the underlying stock if it reaches the strike price before the deadline. You aren't obligated to buy it – if you choose not to, all you have lost is the premium you paid for that right.

The best-case scenario for you, as the buyer, is that the stock suddenly starts rising at a high speed before the deadline arrives. You want it to go beyond the strike price so that, when it comes time to exercise your right, you are purchasing your stock at a lower rate than it is now worth. Obviously, you then have the option to instantly list that stock as a covered sell, which would allow you to realize that profit in real money.

That final piece of the puzzle is the important one. As an options trader, you are not in the business of building a stock portfolio. You don't really want to actually own those shares – you want to make a profit on them as they pass through your hands. You want to buy them for less than they are worth and then sell them on, perhaps even for more than they are worth if you are lucky. It's within that transaction your money will be made.

Buying calls has several advantages for you as an options trader:

- It doesn't cost much to get involved in the movement of a particular stock. You only need fork out the amount for the premium, after which you can sit back and wait to see what the stock does before making your purchase decision based on actual information, rather than on speculating what the market will do.

- It allows you to make use of the kinds of "tips" that market experts have a bad habit of swearing by. You read the news, you're watching the markets and you have information that makes you think a certain stock is about to rise fast and hard. You want to take advantage of that, obviously, and options trading allows you to do so much more safely than simply buying the stock. If you're wrong, you'll only lose your premium and you may even make a small profit. If you were wrong and purchased the stock and then it plummeted rather than rose, you stand to lose a whole lot more cash.

- Buying calls also allows you to consider shares that would ordinarily be out of your price range. You can play around with the big boys, like Walmart and Apple, without putting a second mortgage on the house. Buying options on those stocks is a whole lot less expensive than buying the stocks themselves, so if you see something on the horizon that makes you think the trade would be worthwhile (a new product or service, for instance, or a change in leadership), you can use call buying to get in on the game. This is called "leverage": the ability to control thousands of dollars in stock for just hundreds of dollars in premium.

One thing to note before you start buying calls is that you'll want to wait for the right time. You are no longer interested in a flat market – this time you want a bull market where stock prices are rising.

What you are looking for is an underlying stock you have faith in – you think it's going to rise in value over the next few months. Let's say you've found a stock that's currently at $50 and you believe it will continue to rise steadily. Predicting the rate of its growth, you think it will be at $80 in two months' time.

What you would be looking for in that scenario is a call contract that would allow you to purchase shares for LESS than the $80 you think they will rise to at that time. You must also juggle the math to make sure that you will not be paying a premium that would wipe out the profit you would make.

For example, you might find a contract option that will allow you to buy the stock at $80 per share on the deadline, with a premium of $1 per share. You think the stock is actually going to be worth $85 on that date, so you would actually be making a profit of $4 per share. Had the premium been $5, you'd have made no profit at all.

Chapter 7. Top Day Trading Tools

Software Tools

Retail traders, in particular, can already access almost the same kinds of programs used by institutional traders. Moreover, many of these tools are either available online or downloadable in the computer. In fact, with the growing popularity of mobile devices such as tablets and smart phones, some of these programs can also be downloaded in these devices. This way, you can trade anytime and anywhere even when you're on a holiday or commuting.

These software tools can include:

Stock Screeners

A stock screener is a tool that allows you to compare company stocks against a set of criteria, which can include share price, market capitalization, dividend yield, volatility, valuation ratios, and analyst estimates.

What I like about stock screeners is they are very easy to use since the parameters can already be provided for you. All you have to do is to choose.

Now I can get more information on every company or narrow my search some more so I have fewer but hopefully better-choice stocks to consider.

Stock screeners can be an excellent tool too to begin your research. In fact, it guides you on what kind of information to look for as you can see in the MORE INFO column. You can save more time as well. Note, though, that not all stock screeners have the same features. Some are pretty basic while others are comprehensive they can also let you run screening for other types of securities like bonds and mutual funds, like Yahoo Finance.

Auto Traders

Also known as automatic trading systems, these are programs that execute buys and sells on your behalf. Normally, you just set certain parameters, and they do the rest. One of the biggest advantages of auto trading is you don't have to constantly keep track of your trading literally as the system does it for you. In fact, over the years, it has become more sophisticated that it can already "read" historical data and provide you with recommendations or information so you can make more correct decisions. Also, you can execute the same commands multiple times in any given day and trade several accounts or orders at any given time.

However, there are downsides. First, there's disruption of the markets. In 2014 over 70% of trading is due to these automated systems. Now imagine if every trader executes huge orders every single time. Market movements can then become incredibly erratic. Moreover, even if these systems are designed to work more powerfully than any trader's thinking and analytical capacity, they are still prone to glitches, and these glitches can be disastrous. For example, it can place large orders that you don't want to in the first place.

Streaming Quotes

You can also consider this as your equivalent to a ticker tape. The only difference is that you'll get more information from streaming quotes.

Now streaming quotes are quotes displayed in real time, so don't be surprised if the numbers tend to change very fast for certain stocks. It only goes to show that the market is definitely active. For a day trader, streaming quotes are a valuable tool as they can help you make decisions including corrections on the fly. You can spot emerging buying and selling trends and analyze real-time charts. NASDAQ has an example of a streaming quote, although it's much simpler than the others like Quotestream or Scottrader.

Live Market Analysis

Although technical analysis is essential in day trading, you should also not neglect fundamental analysis as the latter can even dictate the results of the former. For this reason, I also use Live Market Analysis.

Live Market Analysis is simply a collection of any information, news, press releases, and reports pertaining to the companies that are being traded. They may not be directly related to finance (e.g., news about mergers or acquisitions) but they can influence stock price movement within the day.

You can source the analysis online such as Yahoo or Google Finance.

Stop Loss Management

I hope I've already established the fact that stop loss is incredibly important as part of your risk management strategy.

In this section, I want to help you answer a fundamental question: where else can I place my stop-loss order? Learning Markets gives us two more options. These are the support and moving average methods.

Support levels refer to the level in which stock price dips the lowest before it goes high up. When you look at a fall below the uptrend is the support level. In the support method, your stop loss can be placed just a bit below than the previous support level as this assumes that going below the stop-loss price means a continuous or longer downtrend for the stock.

Investopedia, on the other hand, has a good definition of moving averages. One of the benefits of this is that it cancels out "noise" or fluctuations that may not be that consistent. In other words, it gives you a clear picture of the possible movement of stock prices. For the stop loss setup, you can determine the moving average and have it just below the moving average.

Penny Stock Level 2 Quotes

Once in a while, day traders look for a penny stock, although the name can be a misnomer since, according to the Securities and Exchange Commission (SEC), these stocks are those that have less than $5 per share value.

Some traders like penny stocks because there's a lot of room for appreciation, which means opportunities for massive return. Moreover, a person's capital can go a long way with penny stocks. For example, if a person has $5,000, he can allocate $1,000 for penny stocks worth $3 each. This means he gets 300 shares (rounded off to the nearest hundreds). Compare that if he uses the same amount to buy shares worth $5.

However, there are several downsides with penny stocks. One, they are hard to come by and they are thinly traded. Therefore, there's not much technical information you can use to make good decisions about them. Second, they are usually not found in major exchanges because they have failed to meet some of the requirements or criteria. You may also have issues with liquidity, which means you may not be able to sell the stock quickly simply because penny stocks themselves are not that liquid.

Nevertheless, if you want to give penny stocks a try, you can use Level 2 Quotes, which is obviously higher than the level 1 quote, which includes the streaming quote. An important data available in level 2 quote is that of the market maker or those who have significant control of the market, including the brokerage firms. They are the ones who have massive volumes of order sizes, which they are going to trade. Market makers meant to earn a profit, so orders may be hold off until they know they can make a gain. Traders in level 1, however, wouldn't know that. In level 2 quotes, traders can observe movements of money makers and see what stocks they have the most interest.

Chapter 8. Picking Out Some Good Strategies to Use with Options Trading

One of the first things that you will need to do once you decide to enter the market is pick out a good strategy to use. This strategy is so important because it helps you to know when to enter the market, what to look for in the market, and even when you should leave the market. When it comes to options trading, there are actually quite a few strategies that you can choose to work with. Some of the best choices in strategies include:

Tip 11: Working with a fundamental analysis

The first strategy we are going to take a look at is the fundamental analysis. This is a method that doesn't spend so much time looking at the charts as some of the others. Instead, the trader who uses this is trying to find an underlying asset that they believe to be undervalued at the time, for some reason or another. They hope that once they find it, they will be able to do a fundamental analysis to determine whether the price of this security is going to go up.

There are many things that you need to look at when it comes to a fundamental analysis. Understanding why the asset is undervalued is important as well. As a fundamental analyst, you will take a look at the debt ratio the company has, how long it has been in business, whether it has seen an increase in profits over the past five years, whether it is growing, who manages the business, and so on. The hope is to find an asset that is undervalued, and then purchase it before public opinion changes and the price goes up.

This one can help you to find some securities early while they are still at a discount price. But there is a catch. Many times the price of the security is there for a reason and some of the lower ones are there because they are seen as junk or because the company wasn't able to manage their debts very well. You have to be careful when utilizing this kind of strategy to make sure that it will actually work for you.

The fundamental analysis can take some time to learn how to work with. There are a lot of different factors that you need to work with. You aren't just looking through the charts of a stock or security and where it has gone in the past, even though this is important as well. But you also have to look more at the basics of the company and see how it is doing.

For example, with a fundamental analysis, you need to be able to look at the company and see how its management is doing. If there are any big changes in the management, then you have to look and see how this is going to shake up the industry and how investors are going to respond. If the change is because one of the board members just decided to retire, it isn't a big deal. But if there were some scandals and other issues and that caused the change in the management, then this can be really difficult to work with and may show that the stock isn't going to go up soon.

You should also look at the debt to income ratio of the company. If the company is taking on too much debt, it means that they won't be able to pay their shareholders, and the value may go down. But the reason of the debt accumulation can matter. If the company did a recent expansion, or purchased some expensive equipment to help them grow, then this is a good thing and the price of the stock should go up shortly.

But, it can also go the other way. If the company took on too much debt because of mismanagement or they just can't seem to make enough to pay down regular debts and the paychecks to their employees, this is going to show poorly on the company. If this is what you are seeing with the company, then it may be time to switch and look for some other securities to work with.

These are just two of the main points that you are going to need to look into when you want to do a fundamental analysis with options. It is a method that a lot of people like to use, but often it is going to be done at the same time as the fundamental analysis, rather than doing it on its own. Many traders like the fundamental analysis because it helps them to find an underlying security that is doing poorly but should turn around soon, but they still like to have some of the technical analysis in place to help them see more about the security.

Tip 12: Working with a technical analysis

For most of the strategies we will explore, you will employ a technical analysis. The technical analysis can be a great option because it relies on research of the charts and the history of a particular option. It assumes that all of the other information about the company, including its work, public perception, and anything else explored in a fundamental analysis, is already accounted for in the price.

This can make things a bit easier for you. You get the benefit of just looking at the charts for that underlying asset to make your decisions. You can look at how it has behaved in the past, and bring in current news events to see if it is likely the asset will continue on with its current trajectory or move a different way. From this information, you can pick out the right technical analysis strategy and then enter the market when you are ready.

Before using this strategy, make sure that you are ready and you fully understand the way that it should work. Have lots of charts to back you up, and some good news sources so you can pay attention to anything that may affect the current market for the options you are in.

A technical analysis is going to be a type of trading strategy that is going to evaluate the investments and then identify the trading opportunities that come with that.

Unlike what we saw with the fundamental analysis, or those who like to look at the intrinsic value of the company, a technical analyst is going to focus on some of the patterns that come with price movements, trading signals, and other charting tools to help evaluate how weak or strong the security is at that particular time.

You are able to work with a technical analysis on any kind of security, as long as it has a historical type of trading data that you can look through. This means that you are able to use it with any security such as stocks, commodities, fixed income, currencies, futures, and other types of securities. All of the different strategies that we are going to talk about below will work on the idea of a technical analysis as well, which means that there are plenty of opportunities for you to utilize the tools with this method.

The technical analysis can be a really great way for you to invest and see some great results. Some of the different key takeaways that you can consider when it comes to a technical analysis includes:

1. This kind of strategy is going to ask the trader to evaluate the different investments they want to work with and then identify some of the best trading opportunities in price trends and various patterns that are found on the charts.

2. The analysts and traders who use this method believe that the past activity of that security, and any price changes that occur with that security, can be valuable because they indicate the price movements that security is going to see in the future.

3. A technical analysis is often going to be contrasted against a fundamental analysis. Sometimes the two of these are used together to really help the trader figure out the right securities to trade in order to get a good deal on the security, and to figure out

which direction it is going to take in the future.

4.

Chapter 9. When to enter and exit the trade

When you were a kid, did you ever play double Dutch jump rope? Double Dutch is where two people are swinging two ropes and a third person has to jump in for a bit before jumping out. As a kid, it was brutal and difficult to find the right timing to jump in without getting hit with a rope. Entering into a trade can be just as nerve-wracking. You can be setting up to enter the trade and stress yourself with questions like, "Do I jump in now? How about now?" But with some strategic planning, and practice, you can find the best area you would like to jump in on a regular basis.

The entry point in a trade is the point at which you want to buy an asset. It's the starting bid in your trade. Whether you are trading stocks or options, you will always have to have an entry point. Having a good plan for when you will enter into a trade is really beneficial because it means that you won't have to drive yourself mad. It also means that you won't be making an emotional choice regarding when to enter.

Choosing a good entry point means analyzing the chart for support, resistance, and trend. Look at the past movement of the chart and find the support and resistance. Then, look at the trend. Has the chart been moving in a specific trend line? Or has it been in a stage of consolidation? Or a period where the market has remained fairly steady? With a stock that has a trend line, you can choose a point right after a rebound. For example, let's say stock ABC was trading at $60 in November before dropping to $58. As the number starts to rise again, you can see if the chart seems like it's going to return to trend. If yes, then you can place your entry point at $60 and wait to see if the trend will continue upward.

In the case of a stock that is at a stage of neutral movement, then your support and resistance lines will be horizontal and the chart will remain between those two lines. In this case, follow the pattern of the previous movement and again place your entry point at the price where a rebound is likely to happen. This should be close to the support line. There's a good chance that the stock value will rise again towards the resistance in this case.

Let's put this into action. Chose two different practice charts. One should have a stock that is trending upwards, and one should have stock that is steady and isn't trending in a particular direction. Taking the one that is trending upward, draw the trend line in the support line position. From there, choose a position that offers you a small swing up. At what point would you enter the swing? At what price point? How long would you remain in the swing? Do the same for the chart that is remaining steady. What point above the support line would you enter into the trade? It's easy to do this with past charts because everything is already lined up. But take the time to analyze the chart. What makes specific swings more successful and what makes them unsuccessful?

Now try with a practice future trade. Again, find a chart from a stock that you would be interested in purchasing. Map out your lines, find the zone you'll trade in, and then choose an entry point either in the present or the future. After that, watch the stock for the next several days. Would your trade have panned out? If yes, why? And if no, why not? All of this practice gives you the opportunity to try out trades before investing any capital into it. Once you feel a bit more confident about entry points, move on to learn about exit points.

When you enter into the trade, you need to make sure that your risk/reward ratio makes the trade worth it. Once you calculate the ratio, you can determine at what point you can exit the trade in order to make the reward worth it.

Now we're going to learn how to exit a trade. It is very important to have an exit strategy. Without an exit strategy, you will choose to leave a trade whenever you feel like it, which can cause you some losses. You may exit too early or too late. It is better to have a strategy in place so that you know exactly when you'll exit. For example, if you determine that you would like to make a specific amount of profit, that's your exit point. Don't go past that.

As you throw it, momentum keeps it going higher but at a slower pace until it reaches its peak. At this point, momentum is zero and the ball falls back to your hands. In a swing trade, you want to exit the trade before the momentum reaches zero. Not at the peak, but before the peak. This is because most traders will be looking to sell at the peak of the trade, which will cause a drop in the market. Selling early before the estimated peak is a risk. It might mean that you lose out if the ball continues to go much higher than you anticipated. However, you will still have made a gain before any reversal happens and you can always buy back into the trend if you want to.

When looking at the charts for a stock, you should keep in mind your entry position and where you would like to exit. If the stock has stayed steady over the last bit of time and remains in its range, then looking at the support and resistance can give you a good idea of where to exit. If you entered near the support, then you can determine at what point you would like to exit. This depends on a lot of factors like your tolerance for risk and how long you want to stay in the trade. Generally speaking, if the stock value keeps increasing, you want to exit before it hits the resistance. Remember, in swing trading, it's all about small gains, not large ones so it's better to leave with some profit rather than no profit.

- With your support and resistance marked on a chart, you can also look for key indicators that show you that it's time to sell. One of these indicators is either if the stock value exceeds its resistance, or if it drops below its support numbers. This can mean that it's starting to trend in one specific direction, but it could also mean that these little breakouts will backtrack into the range it was sitting at before. If the stock value exceeds its resistance and you haven't sold yet, then you can choose to wait until it returns to its range, or see if it will be the start of a new trend. This decision, again, depends on how much risk you're willing to take.

There are a couple of things you can do to make sure that you are not staying in a trade too long. The first one is to set a stop-loss. A stop-loss is a tool that will sell your shares in the event that the stock price goes too low. The other option is to set a limit order. A limit order will sell your trades once they've reached your set peak value. Let's say that the current stock price for ABC is $20 per share when you enter. You can choose to set your limit order at $25 a share. You can also set it at a certain percentage point for profit. This means that at the $25 mark, your broker will sell your shares. This can be good because it can limit your losses, but it can also prevent you from taking advantage of a possible trend. So once again, make a decision based on your tolerance for risk.

As you make your exit strategy, you should ask yourself a few questions. You should know how long you are willing to stay in a trade, how much risk you can tolerate and at what point you want to get out. These three things will help you make a good exit strategy. For example, when asking yourself how long you want to stay in a trade, you can think about how long you want your capital to be tied up, what indicators you're looking for that will cause you to sell, etc.

When considering how much risk you're willing to take, try a few different scenarios. Also, consider what a profit is to you. Is it a $1 per share a decent profit or do you want to make more? Finally, consider when you want to leave the trade. You should have this written down clearly. Are you going to leave the trade once you've made a certain profit, once you hit the resistance level, or once you see another indication that it's time to go? When you've made your plan, it's important you stick to it. This will help you remain emotionally objective when trading.

Once you've made your exit plan, it's time again to practice. Look at some past charts and analyze where you would have entered and exited the trade, based on the indicators like support and resistance, or based on the moving average. Analyze every piece of a move. Why would a certain exit point have worked or failed? Afterwards, try this again with a future chart. You can either do this in a simulation or using your own chart website of choice. Pick a stock you want to follow and find an entry point you think will work for you. Then, using your exit strategy, determine when you will exit the chart. Spend a few days looking at your plan as the chart moves forward. Did your plan work? Are there other ways you could have executed it? Keep practicing, don't just do this with one chart and think you're ready to start trading.

Where to place your stop-loss and why

We've talked a little about stop-losses, but let's look at them in more detail and explore the different types you can use. A stop-loss is very similar to a fire alarm. The fire alarm in your house starts to go off the moment that it senses smoke. It doesn't have to be a literal fire for it to sound the alarm. This can be kind of irritating, but it is also a very close analogy of what a stop-loss is. And yes, on occasion a stop-loss can also be irritating if it's not set correctly. A stop-loss can help you sell your trades when the market turns in an unexpected direction. It's your warning system and safety net in one. It makes sure that if the market is going to drop, you aren't going to lose a massive amount of money. However, sometimes a stop-loss is placed too tight which results in it being triggered during regular market volatility. This is that annoying accidental fire alarm. Even though it can be annoying, a stop-loss can save you considerable grief. As a swing trader, your trades will cover some days and weekends, which can result in precarious nights where the market shifts unexpectedly. A stop-loss can help you ensure your losses aren't too steep.

For most people, the ideal place to set up a stop-loss is close to their entry point. If your exit is nearby, it's easier to escape from the fire unscathed. It's the same way with the market. If your stop-loss is near, you won't lose much if everything goes down the drain. That being said, you don't want your stop-loss to be so close that the slightest move in the market results in you being kicked out. Try to keep a balance of it being set close to the entry point, but also leaving room for some volatility.

Stop-losses come in many different varieties to best fit your needs. Beyond the basic stop-loss, there are three different variations: Good 'til canceled, day-order, and trailing stop.

Good 'til canceled orders sound exactly like their name. In few words, it's a stop-loss that you place and it won't be canceled until you manually cancel it, or when the conditions are met, in which case it executes the sell. They do come with expiration dates as a safety measure, so they're not held onto indefinitely. There are a couple of downsides to good 'til canceled stop-losses. Because they have to be canceled manually, sometimes traders have had it execute at points they didn't want them to. Also, sometimes they are triggered in volatile markets which results in the trader selling low and having to buy back high if they want to remain in the same stock. These two downsides are part of the reason why many exchanges won't allow good 'til canceled transactions. However, if you want one, most brokerage accounts will let you set that stop-loss in-house.

Day-order stop-losses aren't frequently used by swing traders. They're mostly used by day traders and, as the name suggests, they last only one day. If the price that will trigger the day order isn't met, then the order gets canceled automatically. This can set up some investors for failure if they don't realize their order is only for one day so if you are going to use a day-order, it's important that you are aware of its longevity. One positive aspect of the day-order is that you can use it as a limit order for your exit point. This means that once the asset reaches a specific value, your day-order can be triggered to buy or sell the asset. It's more than just a stop-loss.

The final type of stop-loss you can use is a trailing stop. It is set at a specific percentage point or dollar mark from the current stock price. It then trails the stock as it moves. Here's an example. You buy ABC long stock for $10 and set the trailing stop for 10%. As the stock price moves up, the trailing stop will follow up to the next peak. However, it doesn't move back down, so if the stock value decreases, the trailing stop won't move down with it. When the stock value meets the 10% margin of the trailing stop, the stop will execute, selling the shares. This is just a basic example, but you can set the percentage difference of the trailing stop. A trailing stop is a good choice if you want more flexibility in your stop-loss. Something to keep in mind with using it, is that the set price or percentage shouldn't be too close to the stock value. In other words, you don't want a small downshift in the market to trigger the trailing stop to execute. You also don't want the reverse, with the trailing stop having too large a distance between it and the stock value. In this situation, it won't react appropriately to the changes in stock value. In both situations, you can be set up for a loss, so it's important to set your trailing stop in the right position.

Whichever type of stop-loss you choose, it's important to actually use it and set it up. A stop-loss can save you from a lot of heartache in your trades. ...

Chapter 10.   The Basics of Trading Psychology

We associate trading psychology to some behaviors and emotions that are often the triggers for catalysts for decisions. The most common emotions that every trader will come across is fear and greed.

Fear

At any given time, fear represents one of the worst kinds of emotions that you can have. Check in your newspaper one day, and you read about a steep selloff, and the next thing is trying to rack your brain about what to do next even if it isn't the right action at that time.

Many investors think that they know what will happen in the next few days, which makes them have a lot of confidence in the outcome of the trade. This leads to investors getting into the trade at a level that is too high or too low, which in turn makes them react emotionally.

As the trader puts a lot of hope on the single trade, the level of fear tends to increase, and hesitation and caution kick in.

Fear is part of every trader, but skilled traders have the capacity to manage the fear. There are various types of fears that you will experience, let us look at a few of them:

The Fear to Lose

Have you ever entered a trade and all you could think about is losing? The fear of losing makes it hard for you to execute the perfect strategy or enter or exit a strategy at the right time.

As a trader, you know that you need to make timely decisions when the strategy signals you to take one. When you have fear guiding you, the level of confidence drops, and you don't have the ability to execute the strategy the right way, at the right time. When a strategy fails, you lose trust in your abilities as well as strategy.

When you lose trust in many of the strategies, you end up with analysis paralysis, whereby you don't have the capacity to pull the trigger on any decision that you make. Making a move becomes a huge challenge.

When you cannot pull the trigger, all you can think about is staying away from the pain of losing, while you need to move towards gains.

No trader likes to lose, but it is a fact that even the best traders will make losses once in a while. The key is for them to make more profitable trades that allow them to stay in the game.

When you worry too much, you end up being distracted from your execution process, and instead, you focus on the results.

To reduce the fear in trading, you need to accept losses. The probability of losing or making a profit is 50/50, and you need to accept this fact and accept a trade, whether it is a sell or a buy signal.

The Fear of a Positive Trend Going Negative (and Vice Versa)

Many traders choose to go for quick profits and then leave the losses to run down. Many traders want to convince themselves that they have made some money for the day, so they tend to go for a quick profit so that they have the winning feeling.

So, what should you do instead? You need to stick with the trend. When you notice a trend is starting, it is good to stay with the trend until you have a signal that the trend is about to reverse. It is only then that you exit this position.

To understand this concept, you need to consider the history of the market. History is good at pointing out that times change, and trends can go either way. Remember that no one knows the exact time the trend will start or end; all you need to do is wait upon the signal.

The Fear of Missing Out

For every trade, you have people that doubt the capacity of the trade to go through. After you place the trade, you will be faced with many skeptics that will doubt the whole procedure and leave you wondering whether to exit the strategy or not.

This fear is also characterized by greed – because you aren't working on the premise of making a successful trade rather the fact that the security is rising without you having a piece of the pie.

This fear is usually based on information that there is a trend which you missed that you would have capitalized on.

This fear has a downside – you will forget about any potential risk associated with the trade and instead think that you have the capacity to make a profit because other people benefited from the action.

Fear of Being Wrong

Many traders put too much emphasis on being right that they forget that this is a business they should run the right way. They also forget that being successful is all about knowing the trend and how it affects their engagement.

When you follow the best timing strategy, you create many positive results over a certain time.

The uncanny desire to focus on always being right instead of focusing on making money is a great part of your ego, and to stay on the right path; you need to trade without your ego for once.

If you accommodate a perfectionist mentality when you get into trades, you will be after failure because you will experience a lot of losses as well. Perfectionists don't take losses the right way, and this translates into fear.

Ways to Overcome Fear in Trading

As you can see, it is obvious that fear can lead to losses. So, how can you avoid this fear and become successful?

- *Learn*

You need to find a way to get knowledge so that you have the basis for making decisions. When you know all there is to know about options, you know what to buy and when to sell, and learn which ones to watch. You are then more comfortable making the right decisions.

- Have Goals

What are your short term and long-term goals? Setting the right goals helps you to overcome fear. When you have goals, you have rules that dictate how you behave, even in times of fear. You also have a timeline for your journey.

- Envision the Bigger Picture

You always need to evaluate your choices at all times and see what you have gained or lost so far for taking some steps. Understanding the mistakes, you made gives you guidance to make better decisions in the future.

- *Start Small*

Many traders that subscribe to fear have lost a lot before. They put a lot of funds on the line and ended up losing, which in turn made them fear to place other trades. Begin with small sums so that you don't risk too much to put fear in you. Once you get more confident, you can invest larger sums so that you enjoy more profit.

- *Use the Right Strategy*

Having the right trading strategy makes it easy to execute your trades successfully. Make sure you look at various options trading strategies so that you know which one is ideal for your situation and skills.

Many strategies can help you succeed, but others might leave you confused. If you have a strategy that doesn't give you the returns you desire, then adjust it to suit your needs over time. Refine it till you are comfortable with its performance.

- *Go Simple*

When you have a strategy that is simple and straightforward, you will be less likely to lose confidence along the way because you know what to expect.

Additionally, the easier the strategy, the faster it will be to spot any issues.

- *Don't Hesitate*

At times you have to jump into the fray even if you aren't so comfortable with the way it works. Once you begin taking steps, you will learn more about the trade.

However, you need always to be prepared when taking any trade. The more prepared you are, the easier it will be for you to run successful trades.

- *Don't Give Up*

Things might not always go as you expect them to do. Remember that mistakes are there to give you lessons that will make you a better trader. When you lose, take time to identify the mistake you made and then correct it, then try again.

Greed

This refers to a selfish desire to get more money than you need from a trade. When the desire to get more than you can usually make takes over your decision-making process, you are looking at failure.

Greed is seen to be more detrimental than fear. Yes, fear can make you lose trades, but the good thing is that you get to preserve your capital. On the other hand, greed places you in a situation where you spend your capital faster than you return it. It pushes you to act when you shouldn't be acting at all.

The Danger of Being Greedy

When you are greedy, you end up acting irrationally. Irrational trading behavior can be overtrading, overleveraging, holding onto trades for too long, or chasing different markets.

The more greed you have, the more foolish you act. If you reach a point at which greed takes over from common sense, then you are overdoing it.

When you are greedy, you also end up risking way much more than you can handle and you end up with a loss. You also have unrealistic expectations from the market, which makes it seem as if you are after just money and nothing else.

When you are greedy, you also start trading prematurely without any knowledge of the options trading market.

When you are too greedy, your judgment is clouded, and you won't think about any negative consequences that might result when you make certain decisions.

Many traders that were too greedy ended up giving up after making this mistake in the initial trading phase.

How to Overcome Greed

Like any other endeavors in trading, you need a lot of efforts to overcome greed. It might not be easy because we are talking about human emotions here, but it is possible.

First, you have to know that every call you make won't be the right one at all times. There are times when you won't make the right move, and you will end up losing money. At times you will miss the perfect strategy altogether, and you won't move a step ahead.

Secondly, you have to agree that the market is way bigger than you. When you do this, you will accept and make mistakes in the process.

Hope

Hope is what keeps a trading expectation alive when it has reached reversal. Hope is usually factored in the mind of a trader that has placed a huge amount on a trade. Many traders also go for hope when they wish to recoup past losses. These traders are always hopeful that the next trade will be the best, and they end up placing more than they should on the trade.

This type of emotion is dangerous because the market doesn't care at all about your hopes and will take your money.

Regret

This is the feeling of disappointment or sadness over a trade that has been done, especially when it has resulted in a loss.

Focusing too much on missing on trade makes the trader not to move forward. After you learn the lessons after such a loss, you need to understand the mistakes you made then move ahead.

When you decide to let regret to rule your thinking, you start chasing markets with the hopes that you will end up making money on a position by doubling the entrance price.

Things That Distinguish Winning and Losing Traders in Options Trading

Handling Analysis Paralysis

Traders usually start their journey getting the right knowledge. This knowledge comes in the form of books, coaches, and more. Once you have the information, the next step is to take it and use it in the market. The lucky ones will place various trades, and then things will go their way, while for others, the money will go down the drain.

Trading requires you to determine the right time to place a trade or exit one. The successful trader will know when to use a strategy, but the losing trader will end up placing trade after trade without any success at all.

Understanding the Nature of the Market

You need to understand that no market is constant – it changes with time. At times, the market will go along with your analysis, while at times; it might go the opposite direction.

Accept the Risk

No one wants to lose money on the markets. You need to come up with a strategy that allows you to know when to stop and reflect or tap out. At times you have to pull the plug regardless of how much you have invested in research and your expectations.

Know When to Take Profits

So, what determines the exit strategy? You need to know what point requires you to say this profit is enough for me. At times, it might be dictated by the changes in the trend or your rules of trading. Don't hold on to a trade for too long because it is always better to have some profit than wait and end up losing everything.

Understanding When you are Wrong

You need to remember that the options trading market is random, and you need to admit when you are wrong at times. This is because failure to admit will lead you to greed that might cloud your judgment.

When it comes to trading options, you have various traps that lead to fear or greed. Most of these traps come on expiration day; let us look at the various traps to avoid.

Traps to Avoid on Expiration Day

So, it is the day when the options are expiring, and this is the time you have to decide what action to take. If you are a seller, then you are anticipating this time because you hope to make some money out of the trade, while if you are a buyer, then you are dreading due to losses that might arise.

Either way, you need to be privy to some aspects of trading that will help you avoid any surprises.

Here are top traps that you need to know and avoid at this time.

1. Exercising the Long Option

You need to consider your options at expiration. At times, you can just close the options trade rather than buying the shares. Remember that when you exercise your options, you have to pay additional broker commissions that might not be ideal for you.

2. Options Vary from Country to Country

A huge percentage of the traders on the market use American style options to trade. However, other traders desire to trade the European options and this com with differences.

For European options, you can only exercise the option at the time of expiration, while American options give you the chance to exercise the option between the time you show interest till expiration.

For both options, you don't have to be stuck with the position till the expiry.

3. Holding Positions to the Last Minute

One of the hardest things to do is letting go of a position that you believe in. There are two scenarios under this – first, you have a losing trade that you just don't want to let go. On the other hand, you might have a position that is making you some money, but you think you have the chance to get more money before the options expire.

When it comes to trading, the final few days are the worst times to exit the trade because of the high risk that is associated with it. This means that the value of the option swings in any direction during these final days. Due to this, you can see your profits disappear in a few seconds!

The good thing is that you can decide to let the options go worthless and retain the premium that you collect at expiration.

4. Rolling an Option Position

Most investors are convinced that certain security if way better than another one. Many stock traders think that stock trading is much better than the options because they tend to expire.

If you are on a winning streak, don't hold out longer just to see the close; instead take the chance of closing the deal and making some money, however little. Using the rolling technique, you get to lock the profits in a position and then benefit from the profit. You can do this way early in the trading cycle as opposed to going after it when you need to close the trade.

Rolling gives you the ability to make some profits then use the original investment to pay for another option with a longer expiration period.

Chapter 11. Risks and also the Greek Lingo

When you are looking for options trading, the many types of risk that come up are known as one with the Greeks. Each variable will then be given a different name and you'll find different ways to visit about ensuring that everyone has a little of your effect on your trades as possible. Trading without first taking the time for it to clearly understand each from the Greeks and whatever they mean can be like driving in the foreign country where you were not really acquainted with principle rules from the road and even the language the signs are written in.

When you look at placing a put or call over a specific underlying stock or building your overall options trading strategy, it is important to always look at the rewards and risks from three primary areas. The level of price change, just how much of volatility change, as well as the relevant amount of time value the choice has left. For holders of calls, this risk can further be referred to as either price moving within the wrong direction, a decline in volatility or there not being enough useful time left around the option involved. On the contrary, sellers face the danger of prices moving within the wrong direction as well as a rise in volatility but never when it comes towards the time value.

When choices combined or traded, you will then desire to determine the Greeks linked to new result, often referred to since the net Greeks. This will allow you to definitely determine the newest difference between risk and reward and act appropriately. Understanding various Greeks and what you mean will likely allow you to tailor your strategy according to your individual aversion to risk. Consider them as starter guideposts to be sure you might be about the right track in relation to seeking out the correct choices for you. There are numerous Greeks to consider each is outlined in more detail below:

Beta: Beta, β, is, in reality, a characteristic with the underlying stock and measures the historical volatility of this stock. It gives equal weight to volatility for the upside along with about the downside. When you happen to be evaluating a stock, you can have a feeling of how variable the stock's price is by looking on the β. A stable stock that moves while using the market may have a beta worth of about 1. If beta is less than 1, it tends to lag the market industry, that is often a $1 movement in the market a regular having a beta under 1 means it's going to increase or decrease below $1. Conversely, a share which has a beta greater than 1 means the stock price will move a lot more than the market industry, up or down. Stocks with low betas are more stable compared to those having a higher beta. Examples of low beta are utilities. Stocks which have a high beta include industries like biotechnology.

Delta

Delta, δ, measures the difference in cost of an alternative in reply to a difference in price in the underlying stock. When you are looking for individual options, Delta may be seen as the total amount of risk that currently exists that this price in the underlying stock is going to move. If the strike cost of choices the identical as the present price from the underlying stock, then that stock may be said to possess a Delta of .5. This can further be interpreted as which means that when the underlying stock moves 1 point, the tariff of the option will shift .5 points assuming any devices remains identical. The total range Delta might be anywhere from -1 to a single. Puts might be between -1 to 0 and calls might be anywhere from 0 to 1.

Delta is probably the first measurement of risk that you may always want to consider in relation to choosing the options which are right for you personally. It becomes beneficial once you want to get a put option because you want it to be far enough from your current price to produce a profit however, not to date as to get unreasonable. In this instance, it really is beneficial to be aware of the expected connection between paying less in return for understanding the Delta is going to be lower also. This difference might be seen by looking at the strike price and watching the actual way its adjustments to relation to the put price.

As an overall rule, the less a possibility costs, the smaller its Delta is going to be. Delta is often linked towards the odds that the choice will probably be worth a profit by the time it expires. For example, in the event you are investigating an option which has a Delta of .52, then you definitely can generally assume, all other activities being equal, the option is slightly more inclined than 50%to get rid of favorably.

Vega

When a position is taken, the risk of change that comes from your volatility of the underlying stock is referred to because of Vega. The level of volatility that an underlying stock has can alter even when the price from the stock under consideration doesn't change; and regardless of the amount it changes, can impact the likelihood of profits significantly. The option price is related to the underlying stock price, but opportunity costs are also variable. Vega can be a measure of that volatility, but its implied volatility, not historical volatility as is also beta. Vega is the only Greek trading term with no Greek letter symbol. Successful strategies might be built around both low volatility and high volatility in addition to neutral volatility in some instances. Long volatility options are those that rise in value as his or her amount of volatility goes up and short volatility happens when value increases as volatility decrease. Strategies or trades that utilize long volatility have been proved to have a very positive Vega and those that use short volatility have been proved to have a very negative Vega. Options which may have a neutral level of volatility can be said to possess a neutral Vega also.

As an overall rule, the harder time standing between an alternative and it is expiration date, the greater that option's Vega is going to be. This happens because time value is proportional to volatility because the longer the timeline, the higher the opportunity of volatility eventually happening will be. For example, if a certain $4 option's underlying stock is trading around $90 having a Vega of .1 and a volatility of 20%. If the volatility increases by just 1%, that will be seen by a growth of 10 cents to your total of $4.10. If the volatility had instead decreased, the cost in the $4 option would've decreased by 10 cents instead, leaving a total of $3.90. The volume of change that is affecting a choice having a shorter period is often going to bring about larger changes because there exists ultimately a shorter period the possibility will restabilize.

Theta

Theta: Theta, θ, measures just how much value the possibility will forfeit daily until expiration. Theta measures the rate at which some time an opportunity has left is disappearing or decaying. This number is frequently going to be negative to your purposes. The moment you purchase a possibility, your Theta on that option begins decreasing which suggests the whole worth of the choice begins to decrease too because choices considered more vital the longer the time period of time they insure against new risk. The loss arrives primarily from your time price of money. As a wasting asset, a choice's value will decline because with the concept behind time value. A dollar today will be worth more than a dollar next week. This time decay is tough to calculate and many economic models are complex and sometimes not particularly accurate. If the quantity of Delta on a choice exceeds the Theta, then these options considered profitable for that holder. If Theta instead exceeds the Delta, the gains go on the writer.

For example, if a choice carries a Theta of 0.015 then it really is going to be worth 1.5 cents less tomorrow than it is right this moment. Puts have negative thetas and calls have positive thetas. This is because puts are worth minimal when they may be planning to expire and calls are worth one of the most since the difference involving the starting and ending amounts is likely to be at its highest. Additionally, Theta fluctuates day by day since it commences slowly then builds in intensity the closer the choice grows to its ultimate expiration. This explains why long-term options attract buyers and short-term choices preferred by sellers.

If you happen to be planning a trade that has industry remaining neutral then it's vital that you take Theta into mind, but otherwise, it really is less likely to play in your strategy. Regardless, aim to get an alternative with the minimum Theta rate as possible.

Gamma

Gamma, γ, measures the rate of change within the underlying stock, not the progress itself. Gamma expresses how quickly the option responds to changes in Delta. Gamma is expressed as being a negative or positive number. A positive gamma suggests that adjustments to Delta are going to be correlated with positive movements inside the underlying stock. A negative gamma has the other indication.

If Delta might be regarded as just how much of change that the option will experience when the underlying stock changes, then Gamma can be thought of since the measurement of how the Delta is probably going to change with time. Gamma increases as options near the actual where the tariff of the option as well as the price in the underlying stock intersect and decreases the further below the strike price the price in the underlying stock drops. Larger Gammas are risky, but they also offer higher returns normally. Gamma is additionally likely to increase being a specific option nears its ultimate expiration date. This can be taken one step further while using Gamma of the Gamma which considers the pace the Delta changes at.

For example, if a regular is trading at about $50 along with a related choice is currently choosing $2. If it features a delta of .4 and also a gamma of .1, then, when the stock increase by $1 then the delta might find an increase of 10 percent which can be also the gamma amount. If volatility is low, then gamma is high when the possibility under consideration is above its strike price and low when it's below it. Gamma has a tendency to stabilize when volatility is high and decrease when it really is low.

Rho

Rho is the name for that risk associated with if your interest levels linked to the choice under consideration are likely to change before its expiration. When it comes to choosing the system that's right in your case Rho will be unlikely to factor into the equation most of the time. As rates increase, call prices is going to do the identical while the price of puts will decrease as well as the reverse applies when rates decrease. Rho values are usually at their peak once the price in the underlying stock crosses the expense of the possibility involved. Likewise, this value is definitely going to be negative when it comes to puts and positive in terms of calls. Rho values are more important in terms of long options and virtually irrelevant for some short options.

Find the Greeks

When looking at determining Greeks, be aware that most strategies could have sometimes a negative or perhaps a positive value. For example, a positive Vega position will discover gains when volatility rises and a negative Delta position will go to a decrease when the rootstock decreases. Keeping an eye on the Greeks and noting how they change is the vital thing to options trading success in the short along with the long-lasting.

When you are looking at choosing the Greeks for almost any option, the first thing you'll want to help keep in mind is the final results you will get will almost always be going to be theoretical, regardless of how good they wind up looking. They are simply projections based on a mathematical formula with some other variables plugged in as needed. These add the bid you're putting about the option, the asking price, the last price, the quantity and occasionally the eye. This information should then be plugged into the Greek calculator that your particular platform includes

Chapter 12. Avoiding Common Pitfalls in Options Trading

All successful options traders go through a learning curve before they start profiting consistently. Some of them put in an all-out effort to learn by spending countless hours reading on the topic or by watching video tutorials. Others learn at a more leisurely pace and once they get a grip of the basics, they lean more towards learning from their own experience. Irrespective of the type of learner you are, one way to cut short that learning curve is by learning from the mistakes of others.

This section lists out six of the most common mistakes made by inexperienced traders that can be easily avoided.

1. Buying Naked Options without Hedging

This is one of the most fundamental mistakes made by amateur options traders and is also one of the costliest ones that could make them go broke in no time.

Buying naked options means buying options without any protective trades to cover your investment in the event that the underlying security moves against your expectations and hurts your trade.

Here is a typical example:

A trader strongly feels a particular stock will go up in the short term and assumes he can make a huge profit by buying a few call options and therefore goes ahead with the purchase. The trader knows if the underlying stock's price were to rise as expected, the potential upside on the profits would be unlimited, whereas, if it were to go down, the maximum loss would be curtailed to just the amount invested for purchasing the call options.

In theory, the trader's assumption is right and it may so happen that this one particular trade may pay off. However, in reality, it is equally possible the stock would not move as per expectations, or may even fall. If the latter happens, the call options' prices would start falling rapidly and may never recover thereby causing major losses to that trader.

It is almost impossible to predict the short-term movement of a stock accurately every time and the trader who consistently keeps buying naked options hoping to get lucky is far more likely to lose much more than what he/she gains, in the long term.

For a person to make a profit after buying a naked option, the following things should fall in place:

1. The trader should predict the direction of underlying stock's movement correctly.

2. The directional movement of the stock price should be quick enough so that the position can be closed before its gains get overrun by time-decay.

3. The rise in the option's premium price should also compensate for any potential drop in implied volatility from the time the option was purchased.

4. The trader should exit the trade at the right time before a reversal of the stock movement happens.

Needless to say, it is impractical to expect everything to fall in place simultaneously always and that is why naked-options traders often end up losing money even when they correctly guess the direction of the underlying stock's movement.

Having said all this, many such traders often think they would fare better the next time after a botched trade and rinse and repeat their actions till they reach a point where they would have lost most of their capital and are forced to quit trading altogether.

My advice to you – never buy naked options (unless it is part of a larger strategy to hedge some position) because it's simply not worth the risk.

Note: While buying naked-options has only finite risk limited to the price of the premium paid, selling of naked-options has unlimited risk and has to be avoided too, unless hedged properly.

2. Underestimating Time-Decay

A second major mistake of inexperienced traders is underestimating time-decay.

Time-decay is your worst enemy if you are an options buyer and you don't get a chance to exit your trade quickly enough.

If you are a call options buyer, you will notice that sometimes even when your underlying stock's price is increasing every day, your call option's price still doesn't rise or even falls. Alternately, if you are a put options buyer, you sometimes notice that your put option's price doesn't increase despite a fall in the price of the underlying stock. Both these situations can be confusing to somebody new to options trading.

The above problems occur when the rate of increase/decrease in the underlying stock's price is just not enough to outstrip the rate at which the option's time-value is eroding every day.

Therefore, any trade strategy deployed by an options trader should ideally have a method of countering/minimizing the effect of time-decay, or should make time-decay work in its favor, to ensure a profitable trade.

3. Buying Options with High Implied Volatility

Buying options in times of high volatility is yet another common mistake.

During times of high volatility, option premiums can get ridiculously overpriced and at such times, if an options trader buys options, even if the stock moves sharply in line with the trader's expectation, a large drop in the implied volatility would result in the option prices falling by a fair amount, resulting in losses to the buyer.

A particular situation I remember happened the day the results of the 'Brexit' referendum came through in 2016. The Nifty index reacting to the result (like most other global indices such as the Nasdaq 100) fell very sharply and the volatility index (VIX) jumped up by over 30%. The options premium for all Nifty options had become ludicrously high that day. However, this rise in volatility was only because of the market's knee-jerk reaction to an unexpected result and just a couple of days later, the market stabilized and started rising again; the VIX fell sharply and also brought down option premium prices accordingly.

Option traders who bought options at the time VIX was high would have realized their mistake a day or two later when the option prices came down causing them substantial losses because the volatility started to get back to normal figures.

4. Not Cutting Losses on Time

There is apparently a famous saying among the folks on Wall Street - "Cut your losses short and let your winners run".

Even the most experienced options traders will make a bad trade once in a while. However, what differentiates them from a novice is that they know when to concede defeat and cut their losses. Amateurs hold on to losing trades in the hope they'll bounce back and eventually end up losing a larger chunk of their capital. The experienced traders, who know when to concede defeat, pull out early, and re-invest the capital elsewhere.

Cutting losses in time is crucial especially when you trade a directional strategy and make a wrong call. The practical thing to do is to exit a losing position if it moves against expectation and erodes more than 2-3% of your total capital.

If you are a trader who strictly uses spread-based strategies, your losses will always be far more limited whenever you make a wrong call. Nevertheless, irrespective of the strategy used, when it becomes evident that the probability of profiting from a trade is too less for whatsoever reason, it is prudent to cut losses and reinvest in a different position that has a greater chance of success rather than simply crossing your fingers or appealing to a higher power.

5. Keeping too many eggs in the same Basket

The experienced hands always know that once in a while, they will lose a trade. They also know that they should never bet too much on a single trade which could considerably erode their capital were it to go wrong.

Professionals spread their risk across different trades and keep a maximum exposure of not more than 4-5% of their total available capital in a single trade for this very reason.

Therefore, if you have a total capital of $10,000, do not enter any single trade that has a risk of losing more than $500 in the worst-case scenario. Following such a practice will ensure the occasional loss is something you can absorb without seriously eroding your cash reserve. Fail to follow this rule and you may have the misfortune of seeing many months of profits wiped out by one losing trade.

6. Using Brokers who charge High Brokerages

A penny saved is a penny earned!

When I first entered the stock market many years ago, I didn't pay much attention to the brokerage I was paying. After all, the trading services I received were from one of the largest and most reputed banks in the country and the brokerage charged by my provider wasn't very different from that of other banks that provided similar services.

Over the years, many discount brokerage firms started flourishing that charged considerably less, but I had not bothered changing my broker since I was used to the old one.

It was only when I quantified the differences that I realized having a low-cost broker made a huge difference.

If you are somebody who trades in the Indian Stock markets, check the table below for a quantified break-up of how brokerage charges can eat into your earnings over a year if you choose the wrong broker. The regular broker in the table below is the bank whose trading services I had been previously using and the discount broker is the one I use now. For the record, the former is also India's third largest bank in the private sector and the latter is the most respected discount broker house in the country.

It is obvious from the table above that using a low-cost broker makes a huge difference especially when trading a strategy such as the Iron Condor (a relatively low-yield but high-probability strategy).

Also, it is not just the brokerage that burns a hole in your pocket; the annual maintenance fee is also higher for a regular broker and all these costs will make a huge difference in the long run.

Irrespective of which part of the world you trade from, always opt for a broker that provides the lowest possible brokerage because this will make a difference in the long term. Do a quantitative comparison using a table (something similar to the one I used above) and that would make it easier to decide who you should go with.

Note for India-based Traders: If you are a trader based in India or if you trade in the Indian Stock markets, I would strongly suggest using *Zerodha*, which has been consistently rated the best discount broker in the country. I have been using their services for the past couple of years and have found them to be particularly good. Their brokerage rates are among the best in the country, and on top of that, they provide excellent support when needed, and also maintain an exhaustive knowledge-base of articles. Lastly their trading portal is very user friendly and therefore, placing an order is quick and hassle-free.

7. Getting Involved in Many Trades at Once

Spreading yourself too thin is a really bad idea when it comes to trading. The matter what strategy you decide to adopt, my belief is that you should focus on a few different securities and no more. so what you might sit down and do is pick five stocks that you were really interested in. Hopefully, these are big companies because you want liquidity in the options. Another thing you want is a relatively high share price so that the options have a chance to profit. Know if you are selling options or credit spreads, you definitely want a high share price so that you can earn from the premium. Once you pick out your five companies you should study everything about the companies and know them inside and out. That means looking at their financial statements, knowing when their earnings calls are, and keeping track of things like the volatility, and price to earnings ratio. Then you should study the charts of that company for the past 12 months.

Familiarize yourself with the range is that the price has gone through over the past year. None of this is full proof but you were going to be far better off if you were informed rather than simply winging it when trading options.

So what happens if you do more than five companies? At some point, you're going to be spreading yourself too thin. If you trade more than five at once it's going to be hard to keep track of the changes in the share prices of companies that you are trading. And to decide whether to get in or out of trades you need to be keeping a close eye on everything. Now some people are maniacs and they are able to divide your attention very well and they like high pressure. If you are a so-called type a personality that likes high pressure then maybe you can go with as many as you want. But my advice for beginners is that you were going to be better off focusing on a smaller number of companies that you can really study and pay attention to.

Conclusion

Remember, that risk management is paramount. Always stick to your per trade risk figures and do not deviate from this no matter how attractive the setup might seem. Remember, the odds of success of a slam dunk looking setup and one that looks like a dog's dinner is exactly the same. The market doesn't care about how pretty your setup is so neither should you. As long as the underlying conditions are fulfilled, you should execute your setup in the correct manner.

Your analysis should always begin with the technical market situation which is the order flow distribution and the trend or range situation. Often you will deal with trends with close to equal participation from both sides of the market. This should tell you that a reversal is probably imminent and you should adjust accordingly.

Support and resistance will play an important role in determining where you ought to place your strike prices. Remember to evaluate support and resistance levels from an order flow perspective, instead of looking at every single available level on the chart.

Look at the order flow characteristics the previous time price made it there and compare it to the current order flow to get a feel for whether the level will hold or not.

Screening stocks is a straightforward matter if you follow the process outlined here. Compare the sector performance to the overall market performance to narrow down which sectors you ought to focus on. Once this is done, repeat the same process with individual stocks to select the best to speculate with.

It is a good idea to put all of this into a trading plan in order to summarize your approach to the markets. Think of it as your trading business plan for success. List your instruments to trade, which strategies you'll follow and how you'll expand on them.

The topics covered here only scratch the surface with regards to trading options. There are a lot more strategies to consider. Your next step would be to learn the Greeks and applying them in strategies. I'm not talking about the Iliad but the letters delta, theta, omega, alpha, and beta. You can also learn about ratio backspreads and butterfly trades. All of this sounds very exotic, but they're extremely effective.

However, before proceeding you should master the material in this book. The biggest problem for most traders is adjusting to the non-directional aspect of options. Understanding a stop loss and take profit is easy but dealing with a call option and a short put while experiencing a falling market tends to put their heads in a spin.

Made in the USA
Monee, IL
21 February 2020